EDITORIAL

A question of trust

Rachael Jolley asks why we don't learn that censorship and lack of trust in society puts us all at risk, particularly in times of crisis

49(02): 1/3 I DOI: 10.1177/0306422020936126

THE CORONAVIRUS OUTBREAK began with censorship. Censorship of doctors in Wuhan to stop them telling citizens what was going on and what the risks were.

Censorship by the Chinese state that stopped the rest of the world finding out what was happening as early as it could have.

Surely this is one of the most compelling arguments against censorship that we have seen in our lifetimes. Showing that if we know about a risk, we are able to discuss, to explore, to research, to prepare, and to take measures to avoid it.

As Covid-19 spread through the world, the parallels with World War I and the Spanish Flu were obvious. Here was a dangerous disease that many countries refused to acknowledge, that doctors were prevented from speaking about and that, for a time, the public had no knowledge of.

In 2014, I asked leading public health professor Alan Maryon-Davis to write about World War I and the flu epidemic for this magazine, a lesson from history for today.

He wrote: "We also know that it was the deadliest affliction ever visited upon humanity, killing at least 50 million people worldwide, probably nearer 100 million, several times more than [the] 15-20 million killed by the war itself – and more in a single year than the Black Death killed in a century."

Maryon-Davis identified three weak links that could have incredibly dangerous consequences in the reaction to a pandemic.

One was that health workers on early cases might worry about reporting it (self-censorship); the second was that governments would worry about political/cultural consequences (political censorship); and the third was that a cloak of secrecy might be thrown over it (pure censorship). Check, check, check. It's happened again.

Lessons learned from history? Practically nil.

As we move through the tracking phase of this pandemic, we need to recognise that public trust is an essential part of any response, and that public will comes from a belief in society – and a belief that it will act for the public good.

Trust also comes from a belief that your government will not collect private information about you and use it without permission, or to your detriment.

Historically, those who fought for freedom of expression and speech also fought for the right to privacy: your right to keep information private – such as your religion or sexual orientation – and the right for you not to have an illegal search of your private papers or your home. Those rights came together in the US constitution because those who wrote it →

EDITOR-IN-CHIEF
Rachael Jolley
DEPUTY EDITOR
Jemimah Steinfeld
SUB EDITORS
Tracey Bagshaw,
Adam Aiken

CONTRIBUTING EDITORS
Kaya Genç (Turkey),
Laura Silvia Battaglia
(Yemen and Iraq),
Stephen Woodman
(Mexico)

EDITORIAL ASSISTANT
Orna Herr
ART DIRECTOR
Matthew Hasteley
COVER
Ben Jennings

ASSOCIATE EDITOR
Mark Frary
MAGAZINE PRINTED BY
Page Bros.,
Norwich UK

INDEX ON CENSORSHIP
indexoncensorship.org I +44 (0) 20 3848 9820 I 1 Rivington Place, London EC2A 3BA, United Kingdom

Supported by
**ARTS COUNCIL
ENGLAND**

→ knew what it was like to be in a minority or a protester in a country which oppressed those who did not conform.

They fled those countries to find more freedom, and they sought to create legislation that would mean others could choose to be different, or to express offensive or difficult ideas. That might sound ridiculously idealistic, and of course it was – there are plenty of holes people can pick in the reality of US society – but those ideas are strong, and valid for today.

The right to privacy (and with it the right to express a minority opinion) is often endangered by legislation that is introduced without due process during times of war or crisis.

And it is against this backdrop that activists, journalists, academics and others began to worry that during this pandemic we are, without really considering the consequences, giving away our privacy.

Governments around the world have often responded to the Covid-19 situation with diktats that remove an element of democratic governance, or threaten hard-fought-for freedoms, with very little opportunity for public debate.

India's Justice H.R. Khanna, among others, famously warned that governments use a crisis to ignore the rule of law. "Eternal vigilance is the price of liberty."

This feels like wisdom that's fitting for the current fractured moment.

In Turkey, there are independent thinkers who believed that home was the last refuge where they could criticise the government or talk about a difference of opinion from the mainstream. The introduction of the Life Fits Home app could mean a severe erosion of that private space, as once they have input their ID numbers, the government will know exactly who is where, and with whom.

As Kaya Genç outlines in his article on p50, the question is: can they trust an autocratic state which could save their lives via contact-tracing not to come after them later for political reasons?

This is similar to the question being asked in Hong Kong by those who protest against the ongoing erosion of the freedom which ensured it was a very different place to live from China in the last two decades.

During the pandemic, there have been discussions about the dangers of sharing personal information with the government, and one Hong Kong citizen we interviewed for this issue outlined why.

"Of course, we're willing to do what we can as a collective to stop the spread of Covid-19," she said. "But the point is, we have no trust in the government now. That's why I don't want to trade my information with the government in return for a few face masks."

Another said people were worried about an app that they were required to download if they left the city and wanted to return, asking: "Who knows what they'll do with our data?"

Some governments have put in place legal checks and balances to give people more confidence, and to offer assurances that data will not be used for other means.

In South Korea, a law was amended after the 2015 Mers outbreak to give authorities extensive powers to demand phone location data, police CCTV footage and the records of corporations and individuals to trace contacts and track infections.

As Timandra Harkness outlines on p11, that same law specifies that "no information shall be used for any purpose other than conducting tasks related to infectious diseases under this act, and all the information shall be destroyed without delay when the relevant tasks are completed".

In Turkey there are independent thinkers who believed that home was the last refuge where they could criticise the government

In Australia, legislation restricts who may access data gathered by a Covid-19 app, how it may be used and how long it may be kept.

Other countries have done much less to offer legitimacy and transparency to the data-gathering processes in which they are asking the public to participate.

In the UK, for instance, there has been no sign of legislation outlining any restrictions on how data captured by its track and trace system, or expected Covid-19 app, will be restricted from other use, or even stopped from being sold on to third parties.

Requests to ask the public to add apps such as these come at the same time as we see rising numbers of drones being used to invade our private spaces, and potentially to track our movements or actions.

We also see a dramatic, mostly unregulated, increase in the use of facial recognition around the world, again taking a hammer to our rights to privacy, and ramping up surveillance.

US Supreme Court Justice Louis Brandeis wrote in the 1920s of those who wrote the early laws of his land: "They knew that order cannot be secured merely through fear of punishment for its infraction; that it is hazardous to discourage thought, hope and imagination; that fear breeds repression; that repression breeds hate; that hate menaces stable government; that the path of safety lies in the opportunity to discuss freely supposed grievances and proposed remedies, and that the fitting remedy for evil counsels is good ones."

Those who fear their privacy is under threat, and who worry about other consequences of being tracked and traced, are unlikely to feel confident in a society that takes away basic freedoms during times of crisis and does not put dramatic changes into place via a parliamentary process. Governments should take note that this threatens pathways to safety. ⊗

Rachael Jolley is editor-in-chief of Index on Censorship

CONTENTS

VOLUME 49 NUMBER 02 – SUMMER 2020

CREDIT: Ben Jennings

IN FOCUS

CULTURE

MAIN: In Rio de Janeiro, Brazil, surveillance drones monitor gatherings during the coronavirus pandemic in April

SPECIAL REPORT

 PRIVATE LIVES: What happens when
our every thought goes public

Virus masks a different threat

Hong Kong residents worry about giving up personal data at a time when freedoms are fast being eroded in the city state, write **Hannah Leung** and **Jemimah Steinfeld**

49(02): 8/10 I DOI: 10.1177/0306422020936127

THE RULES WERE very clear – no more than eight people could congregate in public at any one time – but some Hongkongers felt it was vital to break them.

At the end of May, Beijing announced it would impose a national security law on Hong Kong, and the streets swelled with people.

The protests, also sparked by the passage of a controversial national-anthem bill, were the first large-scale demonstrations since the outbreak of the coronavirus pandemic and highlighted the extent of many residents' outrage.

The new security law was felt to be the most blatant violation of the "one country, two systems" framework, which was established as part of the 1997 handover of Hong Kong to give its residents more freedom than those on the mainland.

Many protesters went out on the streets despite fears about Covid-19 because there were also concerns that measures imposed to curb its spread had eroded rights further.

"Since last summer, the Hong Kong government and the police have been trying to cow people by refusing permits in advance, in violation of the basic law, and they will continue to do so, as long as social distancing regulations remain in place. This makes people vulnerable to arrest should they turn up at so-called illegal gatherings, which the arrest of 15 people in April demonstrated," said Tammy Lai-Ming Ho, a poet living in Hong Kong.

Karen Wong, a 37-year-old professional who had previously joined in peaceful pro-democracy protests, was one of those who stayed away. She is worried about joining protests now that the government might be able to trace people's movements and access personal data easily.

"I don't think I'm being paranoid when I say [that] with Covid-19, authorities have the right to stop any demonstration from taking place, even if you're following guidelines," she told Index. "What's to stop them from seizing your phone and accessing all your data? It'll only be easier for groups to be busted in the future."

Wong also spoke about an announcement in May from the Hong Kong government that it would distribute free, reusable masks to all residents with valid identity cards who registered on the website. Even this straightforward initiative raised eyebrows.

"Of course, we're willing to do what we can as a collective to stop the spread of Covid-19. But the point is, we have no trust in the government now," she said. "That's why I don't want to trade my information with the government in return for a few face masks."

Fearing the state gaining access to private information, pro-democracy groups have urged members on private WhatsApp groups to think twice before signing up for masks.

Responding to the concerns, the authorities emphasised that "information provided by citizens in obtaining the masks will not be used for other purposes", and that the "retention period of the personal data is no longer than

RIGHT: Fresh protests erupted in Hong Kong in May over Beijing's announcement that it intends to introduce new national security laws

the time required for the purposes for which the data is used".

People have also been worried about a tracking app that they are required to download if they want to leave and re-enter the city.

While the government has tried to reassure users that the surveillance app poses no privacy concerns, many are distrustful.

"Who knows what they'll do with our data? I've no idea what I even downloaded to my phone. I go to China for work and, in the past, I've deleted traces of protest material from my phone just to stay on the safe side," said Jeff Cheng, who used the government-mandated tracking app StayHomeSafe after returning from Singapore earlier this year.

I don't want to trade my information with the government in return for a few face masks

→ "To be honest, I just hope that the data is truly wiped."

May's protests were not the first time the city's residents have come out to fight. Indeed, protesting has been key to Hongkongers' ability to call for change and is firmly embedded in the city's sense of identity.

"Hong Kong is a city where issues of identity and protest have been entwined very tightly, which is highlighted each year on 4 June, when large vigils are held at Victoria Park to commemorate the massacre in Beijing on that date in 1989," said historian Jeffrey Wasserstrom, whose book Vigil: Hong Kong on the Brink was published in February.

In 2003, an attempt by the Hong Kong government to pass similar legislation was stopped as a result of mass protests. Last year saw large-scale protests in response to the extradition bill, which proposed similar legislation to the new law.

Many believe that the current pandemic has provided a perfect opportunity for Beijing to push through controversial legislation.

"It is certainly an opportune time for Beijing to do this while other countries are otherwise occupied," said Ho, although she added that it was in line with what the Chinese government had been doing for several years.

The national security law could come into play within months. Will Hongkongers risk protesting further given the toxic mix of Covid-19 fears, new laws, increased surveillance and reports of police brutality?

"Covid-19 had already altered some forms of protests and these will alter the mix of activities still more," said Wasserstrom.

But despite this, he believes protests will continue, just in more creative ways.

"When gatherings in public posed a real health risk, some activists, for example, began

ONE COUNTRY, TWO SYSTEMS EXPLAINED

1842: Hong Kong, once part of China, was ceded to the British during the Opium Wars.
1898: The British government and the Qing dynasty of China signed the Second Convention of Peking, which allowed the British to control Hong Kong on lease for 99 years, until 1997.
1980s: China initiated talks with Britain for the return of the territory. A declaration was signed in which Beijing promised to respect Hong Kong's autonomy under the "one country, two systems" framework. This meant Hong Kong could have its own currency, economic system and legal system, but defence and diplomacy would ultimately be decided by Beijing. It's mini-constitution would remain valid for 50 years, until 2047.
1997: Hong Kong was handed back to China.
2014: The Umbrella protest movement emerged after proposals to reform Hong Kong's electoral system.
2019: Huge protests erupted in the summer, following the passage of the extradition bill. These protests led to the bill being cancelled.
2020: The Chinese government passed a controversial new security law, sparking further protests.

voicing their concerns by putting up posters criticising the Hong Kong police and [Hong Kong chief executive] Carrie Lam in the virtual world of the Animal Crossing game, which led to that game being banned on the mainland," he said.

"Now that gatherings pose less of a health risk, due to the pandemic being largely under control – but with the government still refusing to authorise protests that have been authorised in the past, such as the 4 June vigil – activists are looking at ways to express themselves in public in small groups. There has been a call, for instance, for people to light candles in many different places across the city rather than in one park this year."

As for Ho, she wasn't at the most recent protests due to work commitments, but she says she intends to go to ones in the future. ⊗

Hannah Leung is a journalist based in Hong Kong. Jemimah Steinfeld is deputy editor of Index

Back-up plan

Technology presenter **Timandra Harkness** argues that we need to get our privacy back at the end of the crisis

49(02): 11/13 I DOI: 10.1177/0306422020935789

IN SOME WAYS it's a good thing there are no parties at the moment. I would be the person trapping you in the corner, explaining the difference between centralised and decentralised Bluetooth contact-tracing apps, and why decentralised is better for your privacy, and why some governments are so keen to use the other kind to get more data…

If you're lucky, we might move the conversation on to how weird it is that Google and Apple are co-operating to design their own, decentralised, privacy-protecting, software for contact-tracing apps – and how it's even weirder that the two tech giants are effectively forcing governments around the world to use that system.

They want their app to work properly on Apple or Android phones (i.e. most smartphones), because an effective app needs about 80% of smartphone users to run it.

I mean, Silicon Valley protecting our privacy against our own governments? Unprecedented times, indeed.

At this point, let's suppose that I pause to sip my beer and you make your escape. If we were both using a contact-tracing app, the fact we'd been close together would already have been logged.

We might never have to share that information, especially if neither of us is diagnosed with Covid-19 in the near future, but our social connections have become fodder for state surveillance in a way that would be anathema in normal circumstances.

In South Korea, contact tracing has been very effective at containing Covid-19, but it also publicised the locations of Seoul nightclubs where recent infections took place, which led to the stigmatising of the gay community.

While I have reservations about particular uses of technologies, I accept that our social connections have become the vector for a nasty virus.

I would welcome an efficient system of contact tracing, which means one run by humans even though that makes it even more intrusive.

Coronavirus is a shared problem that needs shared solutions, and I have voluntarily signed up for other apps that request much more personal information to help researchers understand and track the pandemic.

But remember the wise words of former Chicago mayor Rahm Emmanuel (and Winston Churchill, and Niccolo Machiavelli): "Never let a good crisis go to waste."

More importantly, remember that those in power have already remembered that. Measures being taken now to fight a deadly virus might turn out to be handy for other purposes later. Further research that could be useful for future pandemics – who could object to that?

Well, some are squeamish about private companies doing that research with data we shared with our own health authorities.

But information about how we move around, how we spend time together and our social networks could be useful to other bodies for other purposes.

Local authorities working out how to reduce the amount we travel. Advertisers seeking to reach our secondary audience by identifying super-spreaders of fashion. Police wondering →

I mean, Silicon Valley protecting our privacy against our own governments? Unprecedented times, indeed

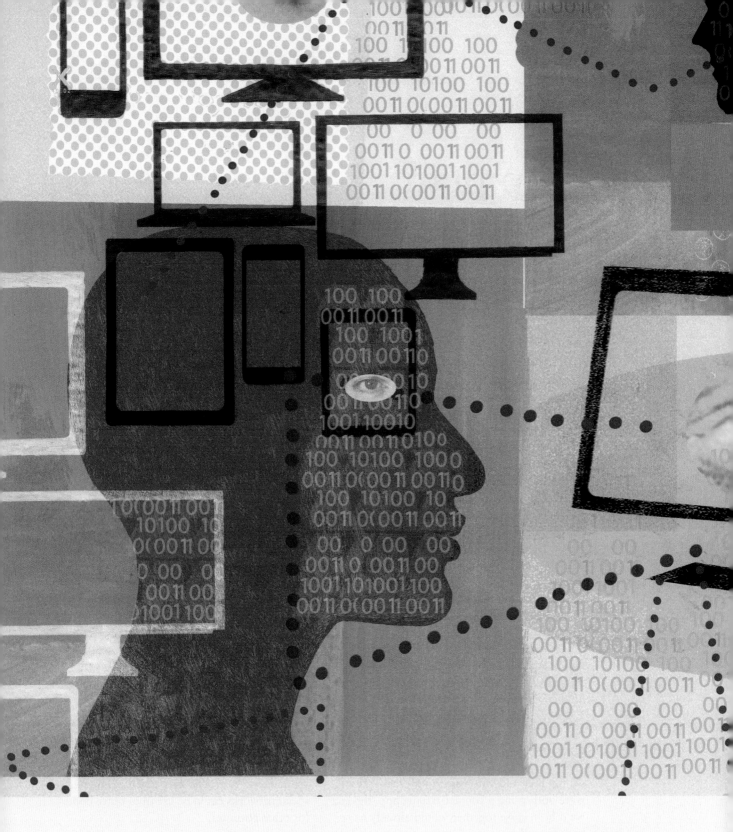

→ who is hanging out with drug dealers and who is meeting them for just two minutes.

There's a danger of getting hung up on the technical details of what data is being collected, whether it's proximity (who you were near) or location (where you were – and, by extension, who else was there at the time), or Covid-19 infection status.

It's always worth asking what data is collected, and by whom. But more important is the question: what controls are in place?

It's telling that Israel was able to implement a location-based contact-tracing system almost immediately because its internal security service, Shin Bet, already had legal powers to track the locations of phones for counter-terrorism

Our social connections have become fodder for state surveillance

South Korea amended its law after the 2015 Mers outbreak to give authorities extensive powers to require phone location data, police CCTV footage and the records of corporations and individuals to trace contacts and track infections.

However, the same law specifies that "no information shall be used for any purpose other than conducting tasks related to infectious diseases under this act, and all the information shall be destroyed without delay when the relevant tasks are completed".

By contrast, the UK has no plans to make new laws and gives no guarantees that data collected to fight the coronavirus will not be repurposed later, even if in only anonymised forms.

This is not helping to build trust among the people who would need to download and run the app, in whatever form it eventually takes.

In exceptional times we may accept measures that would normally be draconian, but they must remain exceptional, not become the new normal.

We should always ask: Is it proportional? Is it accountable? Is it temporary? And if we can't get clear answers, whether from public health authorities or tech companies, we should be very wary of giving away powers that might be hard to take back in a post-coronavirus world.

And at the end of this crisis, what we must ask is: "Can we have our privacy back now, please?" ⊗

Timandra Harkness *is an author, a comedian and the presenter of BBC Radio 4's Futureproofing*

purposes. Unlike some equally intrusive powers around the world, it is explicitly mandated by, and accountable to, parliament.

Australia built a Bluetooth-based contact-tracing app that collects all data centrally, but also passed into law regulations that govern who may access the data, how it may be used and how long it may be kept.

The eyes of the storm

With an election on the horizon and with Covid-19 as an excuse, spies are everywhere in Uganda. It's hard to know who to trust, writes **Issa Sikiti da Silva**

49(02): 14/17 I DOI: 10.1177/0306422020935790

THE STREETS OF Uganda are looking like a warzone. Since the lockdown began, heavily-armed security forces have been stopping cars and asking motorists to produce the authorisation stickers that allow them to leave their homes. Angry-looking cops sit at street corners watching people's every move, while others – suspected to be secret government operatives – patrol the streets in search of people violating lockdown rules.

On the surface, the targets are street vendors. President Yoweri Museveni warned food sellers in March that he would send his spies to catch traders who take advantage of the Covid-19 lockdown to hike prices, in a statement he made to the nation. Fear and anxiety have since gripped the business community. Among the food sellers is Sylvia, 55, who was hoping to raise prices to help her recover lost operating costs and make some profit. But the president's stern warning sent a chill down her spine.

"I'm scared because I have been living under this regime for the past 34 years and I know this man very well. He does not joke when he says something," she told Index in the capital Kampala. "I'm very worried. Maybe we are being monitored day and night by some dark forces out there, and these spies can be anyone, from your neighbour, a customer, a hawker to anybody that you see on the streets."

Ali, a small-scale farmer, slammed the president for threatening to send spies to the market.

"We face huge challenges and he goes on TV to talk about sending spies. It's not fair," he said.

Anthony Masake, of human rights and civil liberties organisation Chapter Four Uganda, said it was not new for the government to use spies and informers to achieve its objectives.

"What, however, is more crucial is what action police take against traders found to have hiked prices or hoarded goods. If they arrest them or bring any criminal charges against them, that would be unacceptable and an overreach on the exercise of the emergency powers."

Many suspect the crackdown on food sellers is just an excuse to stop opposition to the president in its tracks. As it stands, opposition politicians and local leaders are banned from distributing food parcels to the poor by order of the president, who insists food donations have to go through the government-organised taskforce. Opposition MP Francis Zaake was reportedly tortured after being arrested for distributing food to constituents, as reported by his lawyer on television station NTV Uganda.

Every sunrise in Uganda brings further infringements of privacy rights, as a young football player found out when his game was interrupted by police. Gun-blazing cops – some in civilian clothes – burst on to the ground where they were exercising and arrested two of his friends, whipping them and ushering them into a police van. He managed to escape but continued watching from afar.

"I still don't understand how the cops found out that we were playing football because the place where we were exercising was out of reach of the general public. There are definitely some spies let loose in our neighbourhood.

These spies can be anyone, from your neighbour, a customer, a hawker to anybody that you see on the streets

"We no longer have privacy in this country and we are being treated like terrorists because of this coronavirus thing," he said.

Scores of people have been arbitrarily arrested across the country, including mothers with babies, food vendors, the young and the elderly, journalists, LGBTQ people and foreigners, according to Human Rights Watch.

As public anger grows in the face of what many observers describe as an abuse of power, an incensed Masake is urging the government to stop arresting people who allegedly violate preventative measures, and suspend pre-trial detention.

Adrian Jjuuko, executive director at Human Rights Awareness and Promotion Forum in Uganda, believes the coronavirus outbreak has become the perfect excuse for a regime wishing to exercise more control over its population.

"Amidst a cloud of fear, anything goes. The president of Uganda issues and un-issues directives as he deems fit, sometimes backed by no laws at all," Jjuuko said.

"The right to privacy is a fundamental right and, therefore, if the state is without lawful justification interfering with people's communications, then it would be in violation of this fundamental right."

Masake is concerned about how responsible the state is going to be in exercising the restrictions.

"Resorting to criminal liability for individuals who fail to adhere to the extra privacy restrictions is deeply concerning for me. I am afraid authoritarian regimes are likely to ride on the current emergency powers to step up surveillance and other infractions on the right to privacy even after the pandemic," he said.

"Moving forward, there is a need to question the president and the executive on the emergency measures put in place to ensure that they adopt a human rights-based approach.

"Despite its challenges, any lockdown should be under a state of emergency to ensure that the measures are enforced in an institutional framework where parliament and the cabinet play their roles actively – within the confines of the 1995 constitution."

Chitanga Gideon Hlamalani, a regional

Gun-blazing cops – some in civilian clothes – burst on to the ground where they were exercising and arrested two of his friends

analyst at the organisation Political Economy Southern Africa, based in Johannesburg, condemns the Ugandan government's overreach under the guise of managing Covid-19.

"This is done with a clear repressive rule targeted at mitigating the growing democratic dissent, particularly to young people who oppose the continuation of Museveni's stay in power," Zimbabwe-born Chitanga said.

There's a growing fear that the young could become the security forces' main target. The manager of an internet cafe told Index: "People with unfamiliar faces come here almost every day to ask us why the internet cafe is not operating. But I have never seen them here [before], or in this neighbourhood, so I suspect that there could be some sort of operatives or detectives assigned to see if we are gathering people here. I can't take this nonsense anymore."

The young cafe manager was wearing a T-shirt with "Free Bobi Wine" emblazoned on it. Musician and opposition politician Wine – real name Robert Kyagulanyi Ssentamu – is an increasingly popular figure among the Ugandan youth, who are fed-up with Museveni's more than three decades in power.

Many citizens worry that the situation could get worse in the run-up to the 2021 presidential election. More than 20 candidates, including Wine, have already expressed their intention to run for election in the hope of unseating the 75-year-old Museveni.

"Everybody wants Bobi Wine to win because people are tired of this grandfather, a president who sends operatives to spy on his people, including food sellers who are putting their lives at risk to help us during these trying times," one 40-year-old woman said.

→

→ "We are going to see more and more police brutality as we draw near 2021, and spies being deployed everywhere to flush out Bobi's supporters. That's for sure."

Masake agrees. "The use of spies and informers during election periods is a common practice in Uganda's elections," he said. "It often goes further to forming vigilante groups along party lines, and this often facilitates increased rights violations."

Chitanga added: "There is a very high agitation for change in Uganda, with many people,

LEFT: Ugandan
military and police
patrol the streets
of Kampala in April
2020

especially the youth, rallying around Bobi
Wine... I'll not be surprised if Museveni uses
every trick in the book to ensure that he stays
in power and wins the next election, including
using Covid-19 as a platform to extend his
brutal and authoritarian regime." ⊗

*Issa Sikiti da Silva is a freelance journalist
based in Nairobi, Kenya*

Generation app

What do citizens of different ages around the world think about the long-term consequences of signing up to Covid-19 apps? Our reporters **Silvia Nortes**, **Laura Silvia Battaglia** and **Steven Borowiec** find out

49(02): 18/23 I DOI: 10.1177/0306422020935791

SOUTH KOREA

Kim Ki-kyung, a 28-year-old who lives in Seoul, is used to the idea of his mobile phone tracking his movements, so he wasn't bothered when he learned that his government would have access to his location data as part of efforts to contain the coronavirus outbreak.

Several times a day, the millions of smart-phones in South Korea bleat in unison with government alerts that users cannot opt out of receiving. When Covid-19 cases are diagnosed, the ages and genders of the patients are disclosed to the public, along with the routes they took in the days before their diagnosis, so that others can avoid those places.

While the system raises issues of privacy, Kim thinks the potential benefits outweigh the concerns.

"Everyone is at least somewhat reluctant to share personal data with the government, but the tracking app allows the authorities to monitor people who are in self-quarantine, and will allow epidemiological surveys to be done faster," he said.

"The government system sounds terrible at first, but it really isn't all that different from regular smart services, like Google Maps or Nike Run Club."

Kim says he follows the news on how the government plans to handle the data gleaned from the programme but isn't too worried about the data being used for some nefarious purpose somewhere down the road. He feels the more urgent task is containing the public health crisis.

"If no one survives the pandemic, there will be no one left to care about privacy," he said.

South Koreans generally approve of their government's handling of the crisis, including the measures that require citizens to cede some degree of privacy. A poll carried out by the culture ministry found that 80% of respondents said the government ought to track the movements of people in quarantine for suspected Covid-19 infection – with or without consent.

A separate poll, carried out by Hankook Research, logged more than 80% of respondents answering that South Korea's response to Covid-19 was "better than other countries".

A poll carried out in late March, by Gallup Korea, showed 55% of respondents saying that the government was doing a good job running the country, up from 47% in the second week of January. South Korea confirmed the country's first coronavirus case on 20 January.

The country's National Human Rights Commission implored the government to execute contact tracing, and subsequent sharing of information, in the "least invasive way possible", and argued that tracking could present risks such as making people less likely to seek testing or treatment for unrelated medical issues, knowing that their locations were being tracked and stored indefinitely.

Lim Mo-ran, a 42-year-old mother of two small children, argued that her government erred in not being strict enough in handling the virus.

She said she had no problem with the mandatory tracking or alerts, and added: "The outbreak is an emergency and we needed strong measures to deal with it."

Her criticisms of the government's response were about it not bringing in a comprehensive travel ban on all of China, where the outbreak originated, and not enacting measures to avoid a shortage of face masks in the early stages of the outbreak.

She never takes her two young sons out in public without masks.

OPPOSITE: A family wear protective face-masks as they walk through the streets of Seoul, South Korea, during the coronavirus pandemic

Lee Jang-soo, 64, says that the coronavirus outbreak reminds him of his youth in the 1970s when, for a time, soldiers manned checkpoints on the streets of his hometown, Busan, under a system of martial law.

When Lee was a teenager, if he wanted to go anywhere he had to get permission not just from his parents but from the soldiers patrolling the streets who would badger him about where he was going, whom he planned to meet and when he would return.

The quiet streets in Busan, on South Korea's southern coast, remind him of those days. But he points out one important difference between the two eras.

> *If no one survives the pandemic, there will be no one left to care about privacy*

Nowadays, Korea is a democracy, and citizens have legal ways of resisting if they feel their government is overreaching.

"Our country has controlled the virus because the government has been organised, and to be organised they need to have data, they need to know where infected people are," he said.

He then proffered a line that Koreans often use when presented with challenging circumstances: "We just have to endure."

SPAIN

People we spoke to in Spain were more concerned about the use of personal information collected by monitoring apps than those in other countries.

The main conclusion drawn from the interviews is that people do not trust the system completely and fear data might be misused by the government and private companies – perhaps because some people have memories of what it was like living under the General Franco dictatorship.

Juan Giménez, 28, agrees with using these apps "only for controlling the spread of the virus". Cristina Morales, 26, considers it "a violation of privacy but, at the same time, it is appropriate to guarantee citizens' safety and prevent confinement violations".

Ana Corral, 22, said: "[It is] OK as long as we know which information is used, exactly how it will be used and where the data is saved. If the goal is to know if you might be infected or have been infected, that is fine."

Some also mention social good as a priority.

"There are always individual sacrifices for the common good," said Manuel Noguera, 40.

For Eduardo Manjavacas, also 40, "the end justifies the means".

Amelia Rustina, 30, said: "Everything made for a global good and with a clear privacy policy is welcome. We live in a digital age; our data is studied daily for commercial purposes."

And Sabina Urraca, 36, is ready for that sacrifice. "I would like to trust individual responsibility, but I don't."

On the other hand, older people are more reluctant, and many claim they would not register with these apps at all.

For Sofía Navarro, 74, the apps are "an invasion of people's privacy and coerce personal freedoms". Navarro would not even register momentarily, because "my medical or identity data are one thing, but when I go out, and where I go, is the little freedom I have left".

Antonio Cano, 69, worries his movements are stored and used improperly.

"The data protection law exists to protect us from that," he said.

Inmaculada Ramírez, 61, said: "In the long run, this is a way of manipulating us even more."

Among those interviewees who would register, there is a common desire that the use of data is only temporary.

"Once the pandemic ends, both collected data and monitoring systems should disappear," said Giménez.

"I would register momentarily as long as the data is deleted once everything is over," added Corral.

Miguel Rubio, 50, believes it must prove "that once the pandemic is controlled, our data will be automatically erased and we will be unsubscribed".

This is due to concerns that data might be used after the pandemic expires and there is a widespread mistrust in the system.

Rubén Morales, 39, fears that the system may be hacked and used for other purposes. "Once you give way in privacy, it is difficult to go back."

"In the USA, [much] data provided

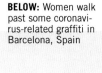

BELOW: Women walk past some coronavirus-related graffiti in Barcelona, Spain

online is transferred to the FBI. I suspect the CNI – National Intelligence Centre – will do something similar," he added.

The motives for tracking are being questioned across the generations.

Francisco Tomás, 63, said: "I do not see anything positive. I don't want the government to control my movements."

And Carmen Seva, 32, asked: "Who would invest in developing an app from which valuable data cannot be collected?

"I don't trust political institutions. I do not believe any measure is suggested for the common good rather than for the perpetuation of power."

On the other hand, respondents believe that controlling the virus does not necessarily entail controlling citizens' movements.

For Guillermina Ortega, 38, "testing the population is essential; controlling our movements is unnecessary and dangerous".

ITALY

The Italians trust the government – but with some caution.

They believe that giving up part of their privacy is a negotiable asset to protect public health and they want more reassurances on the functioning of the tracking app, wishing to know who will keep the sensitive data after the end of the pandemic.

Index spoke to 50 Italian citizens aged between 20 and 60 – in different parts of the country, in different professions and from different backgrounds – about their thoughts on the Immuni tracking app announced by the Italian government as part of its approach to Covid-19.

The app was preceded by a similar experiment in the Italian region most affected by the pandemic, Lombardy, where some of the interviewees live.

Federica Magistro, 22, a university student, and Anna Pesco, 60, a teacher, living in Milan, downloaded the app in Lombardy and are currently using it. They also plan to use the national app. Both hope that the remaining 60% of Italians also think the same way, so it maximises its use across the entire population.

Magistro said: "I think I should trust those who are developing it and the government

Testing the population is essential; controlling our movements is unnecessary and dangerous

that offers it." Pesco added: "I would like maximum transparency and I would like to have an absolute guarantee on the deletion of my data at the end of the pandemic."

Another teacher, Maia Pirovano, 63, said: "Downloading is an act of responsibility, as long as it really works." And Giusi Pappalardo, 50, who works in communications, said: "I have no worries about tracking, after all I use a pedometer and GPS when I run. Rather, I wonder how this app can be functional if it is not accompanied by serological tests for the whole population. If you don't know you are positive – if you are asymptomatic even – how do you answer the questions the app asks you? And if you can't answer, in the end, what is this app for?"

The same questions are also asked by Francesco Castagna, 25, an LGBTQ activist from Rome, who believes the app would be of great collective help.

"The LGBTQ community is not addressing this issue for the first time: HIV risk has trained us. We are used to declaring our condition of positivity openly, in the interest of the whole community. We are also used to living suspended in time, waiting to know if we could be positive or not," he said.

"And, personally, I believe that the Italian app is not intrusive. After all, if you entrust Tinder with intimate data such as your sexual preferences and a declared positivity, I don't see any problem in sharing data using an app of such great importance for the whole national community."

Alessandro Lozza, 56, a neurologist, sees only good things: "This app has no accessible identifier, because it produces a Qcode that is associated with the phone number and does not even have a positive outbreaks navigator, like the South Korean model. →

→ "On the contrary, it will have the advantage of mapping the contacts of each patient, eliminating mountains of paperwork, bureaucracy, self-certification and cross-checks between the national health system and law enforcement agencies who do not always manage to work together."

Lozza, who travels a lot, thinks developing a European app would create a roaming health passport. "If the data were shared across Europe, we could also avoid bureaucracy at the borders, and we would facilitate travelling more easily."

Lawyer Francesco Bonanno, 46, is not worried about the privacy implications.

"The purpose of data collection is of such public importance that the problem does not arise," he said.

Italians are not all so optimistic or confident, however. Marina Fichera, 50, a manager, worries about data being used locally.

Testing the population is essential; controlling our movements is unnecessary and dangerous

[George] Orwell's predictions. Art is a predictive science. I would be inclined not to download an app that tomorrow could turn into a boomerang in the wrong hands."

Gianna Pasi, a nurse, is also sceptical about downloading the app. "I know certain tracking mechanisms so well that I have no desire to voluntarily join one more," she said.

It would seem that those with experience of countries where state control over citizens is far more stringent have more serious concerns about being tracked.

Marta Ottaviani, 40, a journalist who used to work in Turkey, will not download the app. "We ask ourselves what could become of the health data associated with a particular ethnic group or a religious minority if some xenophobic parties came to government," she said.

And Marta Bellingreri, 30, a researcher, has just recovered after a two-month fight against Covid-19.

She said: "No, although I have been positive – and now I am healed – I will not download it. I don't think that after 55 days of total isolation this app will help me psychologically. I only count on individual and collective responsibility."

Carola Frediani, 40, a cybersecurity expert, is also cautious, believing security is key to making it more acceptable to people.

"If the management of the data obtained with the app will be completely decentralised on different servers, and the data protected with anonymisation systems to also prevent possible cyber-attacks, it will be an acceptable operation." ⊗

"I feel quite confident about my data being held by the national government but, for example, I have not downloaded the app of the Lombardy region because I have no confidence in the regional executive, in the hands of the right-wing parties."

And Max Studer, a psychologist, also lacks confidence in the process.

"I trust technicians and politicians less than artists," he said. "Let's not forget about

Silvia Nortes reports for Index from Spain, *Steven Borowiec* from South Korea and *Laura Silvia Battaglia* from Italy

Zooming in on privacy concerns

The lax privacy controls that have blighted Zoom should serve as a lesson both to users and to its rivals, says **Adam Aiken**

49(02): 24/27 I DOI: 10.1177/0306422020935792

ZOOM HAS BEEN one of the winners during the Covid-19 lockdowns taking place around the world. The daily number of participants in virtual meetings via the video-conferencing app soared from 10 million in December 2019 to 300 million four months later. But its rapid growth has also sounded alarm bells over privacy, with fears we have rushed to embrace the technology without being fully aware of the risks.

"Zoom-bombing" has been well-publicised. Businesses have had online meetings hacked, while a virtual Holocaust memorial event organised by the Israeli embassy in Germany was hijacked by infiltrators who yelled anti-Semitic slogans and showed photos of Adolf Hitler.

But that's not the only issue. The promised end-to-end encryption has yet to materialise; some calls have been routed through China by mistake; data-scraping saw Zoom users' LinkedIn profiles automatically cross-referenced and made public; and users' data has been sent to Facebook. The company addressed some problems once they were highlighted, but there is little confidence that every flaw has been discovered, and it has been branded "malware" and a "privacy disaster" by security researchers.

With Zoom being used for everything from business meetings to family get-togethers and social gatherings, intercepted data can include our most intimate secrets, private conversations, political views and personal beliefs, as well as restricted commercial information. It could prove invaluable to authoritarian regimes, blackmailers, ID hackers and corporate saboteurs.

There is also the issue of who can demand access to your information. The data of most users with free Zoom accounts is stored on servers in the USA, meaning it is vulnerable to national security letter requests by the authorities there. These requests can be issued without prior approval from a judge, and typically contain non-disclosure requirements.

Meanwhile, the western intelligence community fears it offers opportunities for foreign surveillance. Governments in countries from Germany to Taiwan have banned employees from using Zoom for work purposes, and members of the US Senate have been advised to steer clear of it.

And Google – which knows a thing or two about online security – has banned its employees from using Zoom on company-owned devices. A spokesman told BuzzFeed that Zoom "does not meet our security standards".

But Karen McCullagh, a course director in law at the University of East Anglia, UK, is not surprised by the rush to embrace Zoom regardless of all this.

"The social isolation aspect of the pandemic meant that people actively searched for tools that would allow them to host video group chats and meetings for free online," she said.

New users typically focus on an app's functionality rather than the behind-the-scenes data processing practices

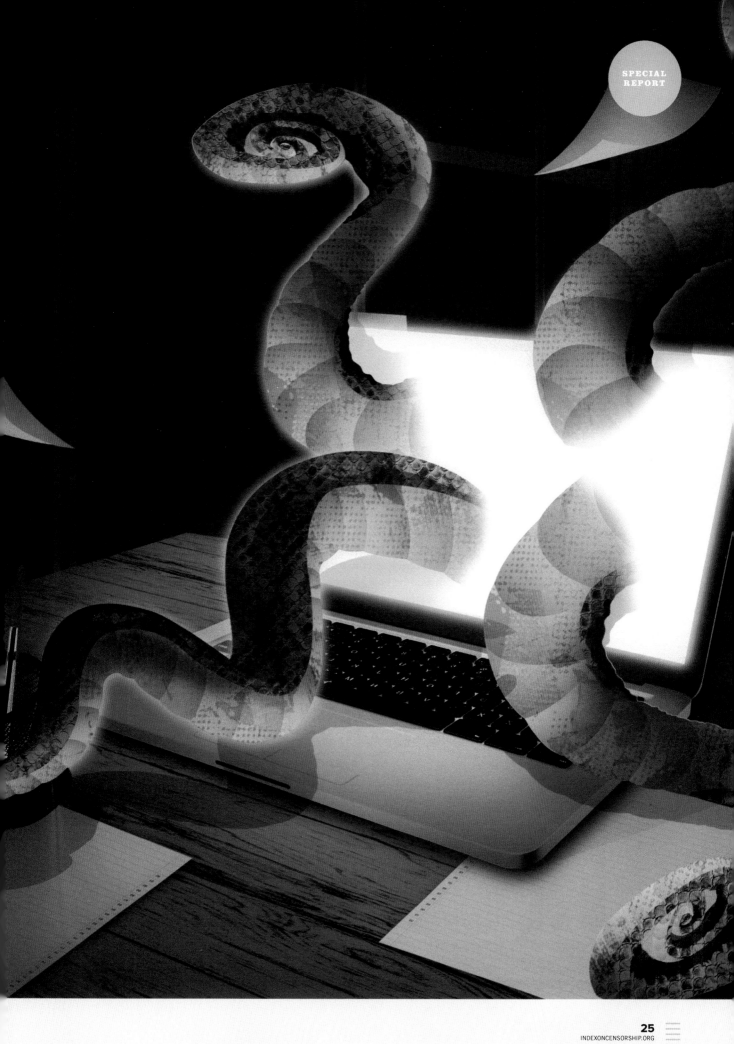

→ "The primary considerations for most people were convenience and cost.

"Zoom, like many other social media apps, is designed to be easy to use. It appears to be free, but that's because you're paying with the personal data you share on the app – something that is not readily understood by users. New users typically focus on an app's functionality rather than the behind-the-scenes data processing practices."

So what can we do? There are some basic steps hosts and users can take to stay safe, according to analysts at cybersecurity provider Kaspersky.

As well as a strong account password, keep your "personal meeting ID" secret. If it leaks, anyone who knows your ID can join any meeting you host. Use meeting passwords, too. And don't share any of these on social media as that could see them shared with thousands of others.

Use Zoom's "waiting room" facility. This feature means all participants have to be actively allowed by the host to join a conversation, and participants can also be kicked back into the waiting room at any point.

And, if possible, use the web-based version of Zoom rather than apps. Kaspersky believes the apps are more vulnerable.

David Emm, principal security researcher at Kaspersky, told Index: "There has been a huge increase in the use of group meeting apps such as Zoom – and a greater focus on some of the problems associated with their use, including security flaws that could allow hackers to access a device's camera and microphone and potentially allow attackers to find and join active meetings. The platform's encryption has also been called into question."

But Emm says not all problems stem from the platform's security.

"Sometimes, people make themselves vulnerable because they store recorded meetings outside the platform and fail to secure them properly. In addition, people don't always review the security and privacy permissions associated with an app or make careful use of configuration options that can keep them safe. It's important to consider security and privacy before using any group meeting app."

Zoom and Eric Yuan, its founder and chief executive, have tried to address some of the concerns. Yuan admitted in The Wall Street Journal that he had "really messed up" on

BY THE NUMBERS

As privacy concerns circle Zoom, just what are the figures behind its use?

9x
The number of times Chinese-born Eric Yuan, the future founder and CEO of Zoom, had to **apply for a visa** before being allowed to move to the USA in **1997**.

40
The **number of engineers** who left Cisco alongside Yuan when he jumped ship to pursue his Zoom idea in 2011. He launched the company in **February 2013**.

100
The **number of participants** that can take part in a free Zoom meeting, for up to 40 minutes.

2,130,000
The number of times the **app was downloaded** on 23 March 2020. Two months earlier, it had been 56,000 a day.

$36
The share price as Zoom went public in **April 2019**, giving it a valuation of more than $9bn.

£1,599
The minimum monthly subscription for the "large enterprise package", which allows up to 1,000 participants in a meeting.

$11
Zoom's estimated **average annual revenue** generated by every download of its app.

security. The company has stepped up its efforts to introduce end-to-end encryption, and has hired former Facebook security chief Alex Stamos to work with its engineers.

David Sullivan, director of learning and development at the Global Network Initiative, which is based in Washington DC, believes Zoom's experience provides a lesson that others should heed.

He said: "Whether you are an individual using such products or the company that provides them, moments of crisis do not lend themselves to thorough risk analysis.

"People use products that work, and it is unreasonable to expect every person to do a security audit of the conferencing service they use to connect with friends and family. This is why it is critical that companies consider the human rights risks arising from their products and services ahead of time."

Sullivan believes that start-up tech companies which fail to allocate resources to addressing these issues in advance should expect to suffer reputational damage that can prove hard to undo.

Regarding data protection, McCullagh said: "Zoom has amended its terms of service

Yuan admitted in The Wall Street Journal that he had "really messed up" on security

to require explicit consent from users, in compliance with EU law. These assurances are welcome.

"Other non-EU based technology companies would do well to note that users in EU countries expect social media companies and app developers to comply with EU data protection laws and will quickly leave an app if they have concerns."

Complaints to regulators can be made about tech firms that do not follow these rules. But by the time that route is taken it's usually too late for many users, and it's no substitute for us being on our guard whenever we use Zoom or any other online communication app. ⊗

__Adam Aiken__ is a freelance journalist based in Norwich, UK

10 million

The number of users Zoom reached in its **first year**.

$500,000

The price demanded for a Windows operating system **"critical exploit"** found by hackers, also in April. It was reported that the vulnerability was suited for industrial espionage.

2nd

Zoom's position in the **Glassdoor 2019** rankings of the best large places to work in the USA.

2

The **number of months** it took in 2020 for Zoom to add more monthly active users than it added in the whole of 2019.

72%

The increase in Zoom's **share price** on its first day of public trading.

$48.8bn

500,000
The number of **Zoom accounts** that a cybersecurity firm discovered were on offer in April 2020 on the dark web and hacking sites.

$4bn
The estimated increase in **Yuan's wealth** between the start of the coronavirus crisis and 31 March.

$1bn

The market value of Zoom rose from $1bn in **January 2017** to nearly $50bn in **mid-May 2020** – more than the combined value of the world's seven biggest airlines.

Seeing what's around the corner

Facial recognition technology is being introduced without legal boundaries or thoughts about privacy invasion, argues **Richard Wingfield**

49(02): 28/30 | DOI: 10.1177/0306422020935794

THE COVID-19 PANDEMIC is the first truly global health crisis of the digital age. As a result, digital technology permeates almost every aspect of society's responses, from people using online platforms to stay connected to loved ones and share information, to widespread efforts by governments to manage the spread of the virus.

"Technology is neither good nor bad; nor is it neutral," the US historian Melvin Kranzberg once wrote, and the technologies being developed now and used by governments around the world could mitigate the worst effects of the virus. But they could also create new forms of surveillance and control of society. Some may even do both. It is imperative to observe, assess and critique how governments are developing, procuring and deploying these new technologies.

One technology of growing interest to governments during the crisis is facial recognition. In Russia, thousands of security cameras across Moscow can identify individuals who breach the rules around self-isolation, even if they wear facemasks. In the USA, Clearview AI, a controversial facial recognition technology company, is in talks with at least three states and the federal government to develop contact-tracing services linked to existing surveillance cameras. And the UK government is working with Onfido, a British company, to help develop a system of "immunity passports" which would confirm fitness to return to work in part through facial recognition-enabled cameras.

Even before the crisis, facial recognition technology had long been attractive to governments – both authoritarian and democratic – for law enforcement purposes. Since its inception, concerns have been raised over its significant intrusion into people's right to privacy, as well as its discriminatory application and bias. However, Covid-19 has given further impetus to its development and implementation, with many tech companies spying commercial opportunities (and seldom considering broader societal impacts).

The concerns over the potential impact of these new uses of facial recognition technology on human rights are obvious. In Russia, a country where the authorities regularly crack down on political protesters, opposition politicians and journalists, the opportunity to use surveillance cameras fitted with facial recognition technology for more nefarious purposes once the pandemic ebbs is unlikely to go to waste. In the USA, Clearview has come under intense scrutiny and criticism for its secrecy and disregard for individual privacy. The technology it develops – which is sold to both the public and the private sectors – works by scraping millions of social media pages and websites for images and videos of unsuspecting individuals.

Concerns over risks to human rights are often met with derision, often on the basis that the technology is simply doing what law enforcement officials would do, but more efficiently. Responding to concerns over

Clearview's involvement in the Covid-19 response, its CEO, Hoan Ton-That, told NBC News that "[a] lot of retail spaces and gyms, they already have cameras. And there is the expectation that you're in a public area, so there's not necessarily an expectation of privacy".

This type of response demonstrates a failure to understand the nature of privacy (and the right to privacy). It is not a right (or even an expectation) that disappears the moment a person leaves home. True, the level of privacy one enjoys in one's own home cannot be matched in more public spaces, but the idea that constant surveillance and monitoring does not interfere

In Russia, thousands of security cameras across Moscow can identify individuals who breach the rules around self-isolation, even if they wear facemasks

with the right to privacy is inconsistent with the understanding that one's private space is not physically limited to a particular building.

Dave Maass, senior investigative researcher at the Electronic Frontier Foundation, a

[Privacy] is not a right (or even an expectation) that disappears the moment a person leaves home

→ USA-based digital rights organisation, told Index: "I worry that facial recognition technology will ultimately follow us all the time and that, eventually, you could just find out everywhere a person had ever gone: whether they had gone to a protest, where a journalist had gone and who their sources are, whether a person had gone to a gay bar, a mosque or somewhere that dispenses medical marijuana. It's the equivalent of a police officer following you everywhere."

It is still not clear if facial recognition technology is even effective. Maass said that policymakers and law enforcement officials were often won over by marketing campaigns around new technology. "I've seen the kind of fanfare that these tech companies roll out. They have huge parties, they give out free items, and this has a huge effect on government officials. So they're being dazzled, but without really being aware of the efficacy of these technologies."

Covid-19 has been seen by some of these companies as a marketing opportunity. "If these companies have a product that they can imagine in some way might be helpful, or can make the argument, they will," said Maass. Law enforcement officials, in particular, are often attracted to the technology. "They want to collect everything, as much information as possible. For them, there's never enough. They don't think about the consequences."

Even if specific cases of facial recognition technology were warranted, it is almost inevitable that these would grow continually. History is full of examples of "temporary" but invasive measures being introduced in response to a crisis, and then becoming permanent. This trend has not gone unnoticed. US senator Ed Markey told NBC News: "If this company [Clearview] becomes involved in our nation's response to the coronavirus pandemic, its invasive technology will become normalised, and that could spell the end of our ability to move anonymously and freely in public."

Markey is one of a growing number of policymakers around the world concerned over the rapid increase in the use of facial recognition in public spaces and the lack of any effective regulatory framework governing its use. In early 2020, the US state of Washington became the first state-level jurisdiction in the world to pass legislation regulating its use by government agencies. The legislation contains a number of provisions which will help to ensure that privacy and other human rights are protected, such as the requirement for human rights impact assessments to be undertaken when the technology is developed, and for court orders to be obtained before it can be used for surveillance purposes. The law does, however, have its shortcomings, particularly the fact that it applies only to government use of the technology, and not to the private sector.

Inspired by Washington's example, policymakers in other jurisdictions are now taking a look. The European Commission has announced a consultation on the safeguards necessary to mitigate the risks of facial recognition. In the UK, the Equality and Human Rights Commission has called for a suspension of the use of the technology by the police until the country has a sufficient legal framework in place to avoid human rights abuses.

But even this increased attention may not be enough. Maass said: "We need to think beyond facial recognition technology to other uses of biometrics, such as body analysis, or even analysis based on the clothes that people wear. There will always be a cat-and-mouse chase as technology is regulated, and law enforcement and tech companies develop new technologies in response. Facial recognition technology isn't the end of the story." ⊗

Richard Wingfield *is head of legal at Global Partners Digital*

Don't just drone on

As drones take off – both figuratively and literally – **Geoff White** investigates just how much information on us they can amass

49(02): 31/33 I DOI: 10.1177/0306422020935795

IT LOOKS LIKE something from a sci-fi film. A drone ascends over a small town's high street, equipped with a tiny loudspeaker that squawks: "You must stay home!"

But this isn't a fictional dystopian future; it's late March 2020 in Neath, south Wales, where the local council has teamed up with the police to issue drone-based safety advice during the coronavirus pandemic.

Drones issuing such warnings have been in the skies everywhere from the USA to India, the UK and, of course, China. It's just part of a swathe of new uses for the world's growing drone population, triggering a swarm of civil liberty concerns.

Unmanned aerial vehicles are an obvious choice for government agencies during a virus outbreak – they can cover a wide area and be used at a distance to keep staff safe. But there are other reasons to use drones, according to one company with long experience in the area.

"One of the things that drones do almost better than anything else, other than maybe a smartphone, is collect data," said Cameron Chell, chief executive of Canadian manufacturer Draganfly. "And because there are so many various sensors you can put on a drone, there are so many data applications you can use them for."

One such application could take drones beyond simply issuing remote warnings and into the realm of spotting likely infections. Draganfly claims that from 200 feet away, its kit can monitor peoples' temperatures, heartbeats and breathing rates, the level of oxygen in their blood, and even detect coughing – all signs that might indicate a Covid-19 infection.

The company hit the headlines in April after police in Connecticut, in the USA, scrapped a pilot scheme to put the company's drones to the test. Some were concerned the technology could be used to single people out in a crowd, but Chell insists that's not the aim.

"It's not meant to work on the individual. It's not meant to hover in front of somebody, get that person's specific health data, identify who they are and determine if they're sick or not, or if someone should come and pick them up. It's doing it on a more anonymised, broad basis."

Chell says the company is "busier than we could ever have imagined" and has had

From 200 feet away, its kit can monitor peoples' temperatures, heartbeats and breathing rates

→ queries from UK security organisations about using the health monitoring technology. This interest shouldn't be surprising. Drone use has boomed in the UK since 2014, with almost 6,000 licences currently issued by the Civil Aviation Authority.

Police forces have been eager adopters. Thirty-five have pilots' licences from the CAA, and between them they now command a fleet of more than 170 drones. The National Police Chiefs' Council says it's up to forces how they use them.

Derbyshire Constabulary attracted criticism in March when it released footage filmed at Curbar Edge, in the Peak District. Over videos of people out walking dogs and taking selfies, the force animated the caption "not essential" in what some saw as a debatable interpretation of the government's coronavirus advice.

But the drone wasn't being used to monitor or enforce coronavirus restrictions, according to police, who said it was "up for media purposes only", to gather footage for a public information film. It has led to a lively debate over how data protection law should apply to such situations.

Aside from data laws, in the UK there are two different sets of rules for public organisations and for private drone fliers.

One is the Surveillance Camera Code of Practice, which says any filming must be necessary and proportionate, and the effect on privacy must be taken into account. There must also be a lawful basis such as prevention of crime, although new and untested laws such as the coronavirus restrictions make that trickier to apply.

The UK's surveillance camera commissioner, Tony Porter, says his office has already been approached by several police forces seeking advice on using drones for coronavirus matters. In the Derbyshire Constabulary case, he says the force would "struggle to justify" its filming under the code, but he has no power to enforce that code.

The second set of rules is from the CAA, dictating – among other things – that drones cannot be flown within 50 metres of anyone over whom the pilot has no control. Police have always been able to breach that rule in emergencies, but thanks to coronavirus the CAA has now enshrined that into a specific exemption,

Some, including those inside the surveillance industry, are concerned about China's dominance of a drone industry that's harvesting growing amounts of data

There's an irony to the increasing drone use during a pandemic that started in China: the country is by far the world's biggest supplier of UAVs, and one name dominates the pack – DJI.

The Chinese manufacturer is estimated by some to supply 60% of the world's drones. In the USA, a whopping three-quarters of 2019 drone registrations with the Federal Aviation Authority were for DJI devices.

Unsurprisingly, the company (which did not wish to be interviewed for this article) has sprung into action during the pandemic, putting its drones out for various uses. For example, they helped spray three million square metres of land in Shenzhen, China, with disinfectant (the company later said it had discontinued the project).

It has also donated drones to 43 agencies in 22 US states, where some are being used for public warning announcements of the type seen in south Wales.

Some, including those inside the surveillance industry, are concerned about China's dominance of a drone industry that's harvesting growing amounts of data.

In 2017, the US Department for Homeland Security said it had "moderate confidence" the firm was passing critical information to the Chinese government – a claim repeatedly denied by DJI, which says drone owners control their own data.

"We're going to have to work out if we're happy to get all this tech from China, with a Chinese [manufacturing] ecosystem," said Doffman.

Nonetheless, supply from China is pump-priming the market for drones, and the current pandemic is feeding into that. Coronavirus may have brought a drone-heavy future a step closer. ⊗

allowing smaller drones within 10 metres. The CAA will consult with the National Police Chiefs' Council before lifting the exemption.

This potentially brings the era of drone surveillance closer to home. Forces could fly drones over houses and gardens, although they'd likely face action from the Information Commissioner's Office if they failed to argue a very strong case for doing so.

While in lockdown, the use of drones is being considered for public warnings, "diagnosis" and social distancing detection.

As countries move to lift lockdown restrictions, could drones be combined with facial recognition to track individuals and enforce restrictions?

Opinion differs as to whether it's technically possible. Facial recognition firms believe their software can be mounted on drones, but those who've observed police use of facial recognition say it requires large, high-quality cameras that would be hard to mount on small UAVs.

There are also more prosaic limitations in countries such as the UK, according to Zak Doffman, CEO of global security company Digital Barriers.

"If you said to people, 'You've been told to isolate, therefore if you're seen out and about we've got drones patrolling the parks etc and you're going to get a heavy fine', obviously that would work technically, but politically it would be a disaster," he said.

Geoff White is an investigative journalist and author of forthcoming book Crime Dot Com. He lives in London

Sending a red signal

Tianyu M Fang reports on when his phone app didn't allow him to leave his home in China

49(02): 34/36 I DOI: 10.1177/0306422020935796

CHINA HAS TURNED to smartphones and big data to prevent new Covid-19 outbreaks, making sure that individuals comply with public health protocols before leaving home. Local governments have, in partnership with tech giants Alibaba and Tencent, rolled out health code programmes, assigning each resident a dynamic colour code based on travel history, health status and contact with known infected patients. This has implications for privacy and basic freedom of movement – something I experienced first-hand.

Linked to each citizen's national identification number, official health code programmes rely on a range of datasets, from flight-booking records and Covid-19 test results to seating arrangements on domestic trains. Residents may also self-report their health conditions, such as fever or cold symptoms, through questionnaires to provide cross-reference.

Such data is readily accessible to Chinese authorities, as public services in the country, including public transport systems and medical facilities, are required to collect ID numbers from citizens – a rule that has been strictly enforced amid the epidemic.

I returned to Beijing from the USA in March. Upon my stressful arrival, I was asked to self-quarantine for 14 days, with my mail and takeaways delivered by the guards of my apartment complex. I was assigned a health code by the city's government. Green means healthy and free to travel; yellow means quarantine at home; and red means quarantine at a designated facility.

RIGHT: A shopping area security guard in Beijing checks the health code on a woman's mobile phone app before she is allowed to enter

Two weeks after my arrival, my Beijing health code turned green. Like other Beijingers, I started going out once in a while, albeit cautiously. At buildings, restaurants and shops, the staff would ask for my health code before taking my temperature, and sometimes noting down my phone number. "No abnormalities", mine read, next to a green check-mark.

The health code system worked smoothly, until it didn't. Before my grocery run on my third weekend in China, my health code mysteriously turned red – meaning "centralised quarantine".

What could have gone wrong? I had followed all the regulations and hadn't visited any high-risk area since my freedom; nor had I received a call from the authorities. I had to cancel my plans for the week. If I showed up at the mall with a red health code, the guard would not only turn me away but might also report me to the authorities for a supposed violation of quarantine policies.

It must have been a bug, I figured. But to make things worse, I didn't know who I should talk to. The interface itself didn't allow me to file a dispute, and after making hours of phone calls to several government agencies – all of which told me they had no authority over my profile and put the blame on another department – I gave up.

I wasn't the only one. On Chinese social media, anxious citizens from all over the country reported glitches on their health code programmes, preventing them from entering their offices. Fortunately, as mysteriously as it went away, my green code came back a few days later.

Technical inaccuracies are only one aspect of the bureaucratic mess. Each province – and

sometimes each city – has its own health code programme. Your code may be green on one system but red on another. While the national government is in the process of integrating all local programmes on to one centralised platform and has issued a national standard, citizens have found domestic trips a hassle as China revitalises its travel industry.

Privacy protection has also become a major concern. Health code systems don't continuously track a person's location using GPS or Bluetooth – as contact-tracing apps in other countries have proposed – yet the programmes in some cities do map out one's whereabouts

Anxious citizens from all over the country reported glitches on their health code programmes, preventing them from entering their offices

through manual scanning. Sigmend Weng, a student in Xi'an, Shaanxi province, tells Index that guards have been scanning his health code, which is associated with his national ID number, to record his entries to public places. →

Without health codes, individuals were often asked to provide proof of roaming history

→ Weng says he doesn't mind giving away his location data for security in the face of an epidemic, but would be less comfortable with it as his city gradually returns to normality.

The majority of health code programmes, researchers at Shanghai's Mana Data Foundation have found, do not offer clear user agreements or privacy policies – a worrying fact for applications that collect a wide range of highly sensitive information.

Citizen databases have traditionally been vulnerable targets for hackers, says Suji Yan, a Shanghai-based entrepreneur and software engineer. Yan fears the integration of personal information across platforms, as well as the information sharing amongst multi-level government agencies, will increase the likelihood of largescale leaks of personal data.

As China continues to build its digital surveillance system through artificial intelligence and big data, such pandemic measures could potentially make it easier – not just for the government but also for profit-hungry tech corporations involved in the data-mining – to track the footprints of citizens over the long term, further restraining their (already limited) civil liberties.

As the country recovers from Covid-19, one might see China's health codes as proof that digital surveillance does work. In truth, however, extensive networks of personal data are only peripheral to China's reopening strategy.

Even before health codes were introduced, businesses and places of work had already enforced security measures, with guards actively taking the temperatures of visitors and asking where they had been. Without health codes, individuals were often asked to provide proof of roaming history, issued by telecom operators, showing that they had not recently visited high-risk regions such as Hubei province.

"The health code is a way to make that existing security protocol more efficient," said Dan Grover, a California-based product manager and tech blogger who has researched digital measures in China's battle against the pandemic. "They already have this crazy patchwork system, in which everybody is using heuristics to decide who gets to go to the store, but now you can make that more systematic and more scientific than it was before."

The government of Hangzhou, which was first to roll out the programme, has stopped mandating residents to display their health codes at public venues since the end of March. Officials in Yunnan province have claimed that health code data will be destroyed once the epidemic ends, although no possible timeline has been provided. Meanwhile, as Beijing loosens its mandatory quarantine policy, I'm asked to show my health code less frequently than I was.

While some cities are dropping health codes, others are bracing for a second wave. David Cohen and Eliza Gkritsi of TechNode, a China-based news outlet, reported more dynamic adoption, with "ramp-ups in digital controls and checkpoints, presumably in response to recent increases in case numbers" in Guangzhou and Yantai – a contrast to the lax implementation in Shanghai.

In March, the city of Guangzhou announced its plan to turn health codes into long-term digital identity certificates, but it has not further elaborated what that might look like.

It is still too early to predict the future of health codes. But if China does want to double-down on its digital surveillance, maybe it doesn't have to take advantage of this crisis at all. "For practical purposes, all these government databases are already keyed on the national ID card," Grover said. "Why do you need a separate digital code and make people conscious of the surveillance?" ⊗

Tianyu M Fang is a writer and journalist. He covers Chinese politics, technology and culture

The not so secret garden

Will we lose gardens as havens of peace, freedom and reflection? The Idler editor **Tom Hodgkinson** wonders what's changing

49(02): 37/39 I DOI: 10.1177/0306422020935797

I **WAS ENJOYING REFRESHING** my spirits and drinking a beer in our small backyard in west London the other day, and thanking my lucky stars I had a yard, when I was disturbed by a police helicopter buzzing overhead. A bolt of anxiety shot through me. Perhaps they were spying on me?

Was I even allowed to be sunbathing and sitting on a bench? I had to check with my teenage daughter, a strict promoter of government rules of behaviour during the coronavirus pandemic, that I wasn't doing anything wrong.

My reasoning self then kicked in and I told myself that the helicopter was probably chasing a criminal.

However, had I been like poet William Blake and his wife, who enjoyed cavorting naked in their Peckham garden, I might have been a trifle disturbed.

Gardens are supposed to be a haven of freedom and privacy in an increasingly constrained world. In the garden, you can be as you like. You can cavort naked, grow roses and parsley, and fall asleep.

In the garden, we can do what we want, when we want and how we want, free from prying eyes.

As Francis Bacon wrote many years ago:

"God Almighty planted a garden. And indeed it is the purest of human pleasures. It is the greatest refreshment to the spirits of man."

While reclining on a 17th-century balcony in the lovely medieval town of Korkula, in Croatia, last year, my repose was disturbed by a buzzing noise.

"It's a drone!" said my 14-year-old son, excitedly. I looked up and, sure enough, there in the blue sky hovered a little unmanned aircraft.

We watched as it hovered near us, peering.

I took a picture of it in a sort of ineffective act of surveillance revenge. It then slowly moved off into the distance. I felt that I'd been spied upon.

Was the drone – a flying camera – sending photographs back to base? Had it been sent by Silicon Valley overlords to take photos of the ancient medieval town for the purposes of gathering free data of some sort which they would later sell to the highest bidder? Had it taken a photo of me doing something wrong?

Either way, the experience was distinctly unsettling and left me wary of the possibility that surveillance tech could destroy the sanctity and privacy of our gardens.

If you're a believer in Naomi Klein's "shock doctrine" theory (that crises are exploited to establish controversial policies while citizens are too distracted to engage or to resist) then you will also believe that the powers-that-be could have used the fear generated by the coronavirus to step up their surveillance operations.

On 26 March, The Guardian ran a story with the headline "UK police use drones and roadblocks to enforce lockdown".

Police in the Peak District, the piece said, had used drones to take pictures of people caught in the terrible and selfish act of walking their dogs. The drone was also used to take →

You can cavort naked, grow roses and parsley, and fall asleep

In the garden, we can do what we want, when we want and how we want, free from prying eyes

→ pictures of number plates which were traced to Sheffield, a full 30 minutes' drive away.

I called Silkie Carlo, who runs the civil liberties pressure group Big Brother Watch. She said that while most people would continue to enjoy their gardening activities unobserved, lockdown had provided an opportunity for further encroachments on civil liberties.

"Drones over gardens is a realistic prospect," she said. "Safeguards around drones have certainly been relaxed during lockdown. As a surveillance method it is now on the table."

That's a pretty worrying thought.

My mother, now in her late 70s, has recently rediscovered her own small garden in Oxford, having not visited it for seven years, being not particularly keen on mud and the natural world.

Living on her own, she has suffered terribly during lockdown and tells me on the telephone that her life is not worth living. She just cannot stand being told what to do.

I suggested she installed

a shed in her garden and she leapt at the idea. Now this garden project has become an expression of her free will and autonomy. Her new garden, with its cosy private cabin, will be a patch of independence.

If she saw a drone hovering overhead I think she would make good on her much repeated threat to "go to Sweden".

Drones are already being eyed up to be used for transportation, and in April the UK government announced that it would be trialling their use to carry medical supplies from Hampshire to the Isle of Wight.

Whether this is the thin end of a large surveillance wedge (who could object to the movement of medical supplies?) remains to be seen. It would seem logical to conclude, however, that the spying industry will be hoping to use drones as much as possible.

The US military already has no fewer than 94 different types of "unmanned aerial vehicles" in use and in development. Their names have a poetic quality to them, I think, including the Northrop Grummann Firebird Intelligence-Gathering Unmanned Aircraft and the General Atomics Predator Intelligence/Surveillance/Reconaissance Unmanned Aerial Vehicle.

The idea of little unmanned cameras getting in your face while you are trying to nod off in your deckchair with a G&T might sound fanciful. But who would have predicted 20 years ago that half the world would be carrying surveillance devices in their pockets, thereby telling Californian techies not only where we are but what we are doing and our consumer preferences?

Enjoy your remaining freedoms while they last. ⊗

Tom Hodgkinson *is the editor of Idler*

Hackers paradise

Cybercrime has risen as a result of Covid-19 in Latin America. Could contact tracing apps further erode people's privacy and expose them to more danger, asks **Stephen Woodman**

49(02): 40/42 | DOI: 10.1177/0306422020935798

ANDRÉ FERRAZ IS worried. The 30-year-old Brazilian entrepreneur, who has spent the past decade building an app that tracks the movements of smartphone users while anonymising their data, has watched with concern as governments turn to location technology to map the coronavirus.

"Anonymising location is not easy," Ferraz told Index. "It's one of the most challenging things you can work on... If [governments] apply the wrong technologies, people will soon see that location data is extremely dangerous."

With lockdowns in Latin America potentially set to last until late August, the Covid-19 pandemic has intensified the debate about civil liberties in the region. While technology can prove invaluable for responding to viruses, Latin American governments have historically proven unreliable guardians of sensitive data. Rights groups have warned that instruments used to track the virus could later serve to break up protests or track down and murder journalists.

Ferraz's company, Inloco, recently donated data from more than 37 million people so authorities could estimate the percentage of citizens leaving their homes. Inloco sent a push notification asking for consent from the smartphone users on its database. According to Ferraz, the platform helps state governments predict the curve of infection.

"We wanted to prove it's possible to leverage location technology while protecting people's privacy," Ferraz said. "If we don't use location technology the right way, someone will use it the wrong way."

Paradoxically, Inloco's developers say they designed the surveillance app to strengthen privacy. The company usually works with financial firms to prevent fraud. If a hacker discovers a person's bank details and tries to log in to their account, Inloco's tracking device will alert the bank that the behaviour does not match the account owner's and it will block the transaction.

Whether used for banking or virus control, Inloco's location-based footprint has the advantage of being dynamic. That contrasts with fingerprint or facial recognition technology, which offers a permanent record. Inloco also encrypts its users' home and work addresses and does not store any personal details.

In contrast, Colombia's controversial CoronApp – a free app the government made available in March – asks users for their names, national identity numbers and mobile phone numbers. It offers a daily check-up designed to identify symptoms. In return for downloading the app, citizens gain a free gigabyte of internet data and 100 minutes of calls. More than four million Colombians installed the app within the first two months of its release.

CoronApp has the potential for contact tracing, meaning smartphones with the app will send wireless signals to other nearby devices, and health authorities can issue alerts to anyone who has crossed paths with someone who has tested positive for Covid-19. After early setbacks with the contact-tracing function, the government now hopes to partner with Apple and Google to bring it in.

Contact tracing has helped authorities control Covid-19 outbreaks in South Korea, Singapore and Israel. But experts have questioned whether the technology will prove useful in a country where only 65% of the population have mobile internet access.

Alongside these practical issues, analysts have raised concerns that CoronApp could open the door to infringements on civil liberties. While the app asks for the explicit consent of citizens, they have no control over the future use of their information. Fundación Karisma,

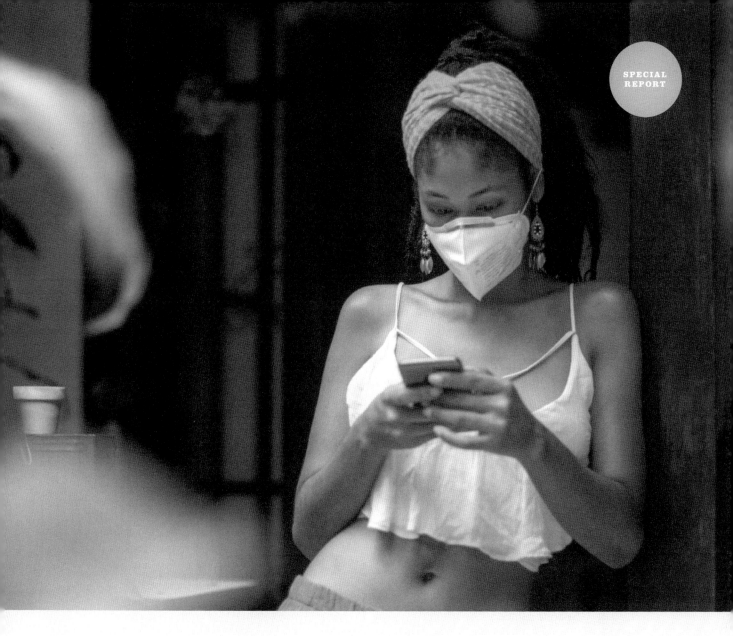

a digital activism organisation, criticised the government for not revealing how long it intended to store the data. CoronApp has since updated its terms and conditions to specify that it will store the information for the duration of the pandemic. However, it still includes a vague stipulation allowing for longer storage of some anonymised data if needed.

Carolina Botero, the director of Fundación Karisma, told Index the government had adopted the philosophy of "it's better to beg for forgiveness than ask for permission". She warned that Colombia ran the risk of "normalising surveillance without even having a debate".

A series of recent privacy scandals in the country has heightened concerns about the handling of sensitive data. In April, the defence ministry fired 11 military officials and accepted the resignation of a general after local news magazine

Semana accused the army of spying on at least 130 people. The targets included domestic and foreign journalists, politicians and judges.

Even the country's National Protection Unit – the agency charged with safeguarding at-risk journalists and activists – has a tarnished reputation. Last year, police raided its Bogota offices as part of an investigation into an official suspected of selling security data to criminals.

Such privacy breaches are not unique to Colombia. Governments across the region →

ABOVE: A woman using her phone in Colombia, where the controversial CoronApp has been critisicised for its privacy implications

Colombia ran the risk of 'normalising surveillance without even having a debate'

A series of recent privacy scandals in the country has heightened concerns about the handling of sensitive data

→ have invested heavily in spyware in recent years. In 2015, hackers published records from the Italian firm HackingTeam. They revealed Brazil, Chile, Colombia, Ecuador, Honduras and Panama had bought surveillance technology from the company.

But no other country matched Mexico's enthusiasm for the technology. The government spent more than $6 million on HackingTeam's products – more than its other Latin American clients combined. And in 2017, digital watchdog The Citizen Lab revealed the Mexican government had used Pegasus spyware to target journalists and dissenters.

Given that recent history, rights activists have expressed alarm that the Mexico City government asks for a range of personal details – including names, home addresses and mobile phone numbers – on its official Covid-19 online screening form. The privacy notice says the data may be shared with various judicial and administrative bodies.

That information could fall into the wrong hands, regardless of the government's intentions. Chile, Ecuador, Mexico and Panama all reported major data leaks in 2019, as governments or companies accidentally placed personal information online.

Data breaches – where outsiders steal the information – are another risk. In April 2019, a hacker broke into the database of the Mexican embassy in Guatemala and published scans of passports and other documents.

Early indicators suggest cybercrime has spiralled in the context of coronavirus. With millions of workers accessing sensitive data from home, social distancing measures have created new opportunities for criminals. The cybersecurity firm Kaspersky documented a 35% rise in cyberattacks on smartphones in Mexico from February to March.

IntSights, a threat intelligence company, has identified "the marriage of violent drug gangs and the underground hacking community" as "a significant emerging threat" in the country. The prospect of criminals accessing personal details related to media workers is a frightening one, given Mexico is the deadliest country for journalists in the western hemisphere.

Vladimir Chorny, an investigator for Mexican digital rights group R3D, believes hacks are inevitable. As well as investing in cybersecurity, he urges Latin American countries to revise their laws to minimise data collection.

Current privacy legislation is lagging in Latin America. Brazil has emerged as a leader in this regard, passing its expansive General Data Protection Law in 2018. However, the pandemic has forced the government to postpone its enactment until 2021.

Chorny argues that governments should collect the minimum amount of data and introduce sunset clauses – limiting the time they hold it. The government must also assign data to a specific authority and prevent sharing between separate official bodies.

While new technologies are rapidly emerging without appropriate legislation in place, Chorny expects few of these will achieve their public health objectives. He believes that when governments begin to update their data protection laws, they may have a better understanding of why respecting privacy and freedom of expression is essential.

"The coronavirus crisis is showing us there are situations in which technology is effective and others in which it is not," Chorny said.

"The great majority of the effective technologies are compatible with the democratic safeguards we are asking for – transparency, sunset clauses, controls. None of these [safeguards] prevents the technology from responding to a health crisis. All they do is reduce the risk that the information is misused." ⊗

Stephen Woodman is contributing editor for Index in Mexico. He is based in Guadalajara

Italy's bad internet connection

Italians fall behind many other western countries on computer access and digital knowledge, so how does that affect the public's willingness to embrace new government initiatives? **Alessio Perrone** investigates

49(02): 43/45 I DOI: 10.1177/0306422020935799

ONCE ITALY STARTED to reopen after the spring lockdown, new words started to fill web pages and debates in Italian media: "contact tracing", "data storage", "centralised" and "decentralised".

For many, these words were a mystery and had little to do with their lives.

Eurostat's 2019 Digital Economy and Society Index – which tracks the evolution of EU member states in digital competitiveness – ranked Italy fifth from last across the EU member countries, ahead of Bulgaria and Romania, noting that "three out of 10 people are not regular internet users yet, and more than half of the population still lack basic digital skills".

In 2019, a third of Italian families did not own a computer, laptop or tablet – and this number is higher in the poorer south.

The problem became obvious when Italy enforced the first lockdown in the west, and teachers and students had to pivot to distance-learning. Eloisa Di Rocco, a researcher with the Fondazione Reggio Children, wrote that, even in the wealthier north, many children had access only to smartphones. Many had to use friends' and colleagues' printers to print out assignments.

And while most Italians would like to delete their data online, according to cybersecurity and anti-virus provider Kaspersky, about half of the population has no idea how to do it.

Digital literacy is a population's ability to live with, work with and think critically about digital resources. It means being able not only to read and do basic stuff online but also to understand how the online world is different from the non-digital one – for example, understanding how tracking and apps work.

Without allowing public scrutiny in parliament or through a press conference, the Italian government began developing a contact tracing app under the enticing name of Immuni.

Many Italians seem undeterred by the fuzzy details around how much Immuni would track them, and the dangers for their privacy. A survey by consumer association Altroconsumo found that, in April, two-thirds of Italians were eager to download the app. About half of respondents said they would do so no matter what, even if the app collected personal data without anonymising it.

There is probably more than one reason why privacy seems less important than health for Italians – including the fact that the country had faced one of the world's most severe outbreaks and the west's longest lockdown.

But experts believe there are also cultural reasons behind it.

"The concept of the importance of privacy is popular among Italians," said Arturo Di Corinto, a prominent journalist specialising in digital rights. "But," he conceded, "people don't really know what it's about."

→

If many people do not own computers or they struggle to understand how tracking works, they are less able to understand how technology violates their privacy

*For years, civil rights movements
have been fighting against digitisation
undermining everybody's privacy*

→ Unlike in other European countries, Italy lacks a thriving environment of digital rights NGOs and foundations that could educate the public, spread awareness about new technology and influence political decisions, Stefania Milan, an Italian associate professor of new media and digital culture at the University of Amsterdam, says.

She mentions the Dutch NGO Bits of Freedom as an example of how a vibrant third-sector organisation could help raise awareness about digital rights. Every year, Bits of Freedom organises a Big Brother Award – an event that brings to light the most privacy-threatening practices by "celebrating" the government and private organisations with the worst record.

These are some of the reasons why, according to Di Corinto, there is a lot of "ignorance".

"Unfortunately, these are advanced debates of people who study," he said. "People are picking up tomatoes for €3 ($3.3) an hour, and they don't care about privacy all that much, because there isn't a culture of rights."

This makes technical conversations more difficult.

"Low digital literacy doesn't favour the introduction of [more harmful] privacy laws, but it's an ecosystem that allows those with an interest to run extremely harmful initiatives without any public outrage," said Raffaele Angius, a tech journalist who often writes for Wired Italia and La Stampa.

In other words, if many people do not own computers or they struggle to understand how tracking works, they are less able to understand how technology violates their privacy.

And according to Stefania Milan, digital literacy and skills act like an "antibody", better equipping people to push back against efforts to take away their privacy rights.

In Germany, where some 70% of the population has at least basic digital skills, and where the debate about technology and privacy has been prominent for years, the public played a key role in the contact tracing debate.

When health minister Jens Spahn unveiled plans for a centralised app that would track the population's position through their phones' GPS systems, he faced "massive criticism" from society, said Daniel Leisegang, a political scientist and editor at the German political magazine Blätter.

Spahn was forced to backtrack and introduced plans for a different, more privacy-conscious app, called Decentralised Privacy-Preserving Proximity Tracing, or DP3T.

"This debate about the privacy of the German citizens was enormously important," said Leisegang. "For years, civil rights movements have been fighting against digitisation undermining everybody's privacy."

Italian authorities, it seems, reached similar conclusions – demanding that Immuni was not compulsory and was to be based on a decentralised approach to data storage, but the public participated much less in the debate. When it did, this participation left a lot to be desired.

On 12 April, Roberto Burioni, one of Italy's most prominent virologists and science communicators and a leader in the public debate about the coronavirus pandemic, called those who worried that the state was overreaching *babbei* ("suckers") on Twitter.

He added: "I'm sorry, but between health and privacy there is a well-defined priority that we need to affirm very clearly," suggesting that privacy would have to give way to fight the virus.

"It's not the case at all," said Raffaele Angius. "The only really effective tracking technologies are also perfectly able to combine privacy and health."

Much of the media also seemed lost, said Raffaele Barberio, the president of Privacy Italia, an organisation aiming to raise awareness about the protection of personal data.

"The Italian press filled newspaper pages because talking about technology is cool," he

said. "But most journalists don't understand very much about these things, either."

While a limited number of tech journalists and experts wrote in depth about the issue, many generalist newspapers with scarce resources and fast turnarounds "talked about it very much, but often chaotically".

For example, newspapers devoted dozens of articles to the distinction between "centralised" and "decentralised" approaches to data storage. But they didn't go into issues readers would have cared more about, such as who gets to see their data, how much their country has to rely on Silicon Valley infrastructure, or the dangers of using Bluetooth.

The worst news is that if governments become more prone to overreaching in the post-pandemic world it might take years for countries in the same position to create the necessary digital "antibodies".

"What is important is that these things are discussed over time, that schools could educate on these issues and that there is a widespread awareness," said Milan.

Di Corinto agrees. "The culture of privacy is slow, long and difficult work," he said. "Exactly like the exercise of democracy." ⊗

Alessio Perrone is a regular writer for Index on Censorship, and is based in Milan

ABOVE: In a country where a third of households don't own a tablet, laptop or a computer, a small group of people congregate on the street in Tuscany

Rowson

49(02): 46/47 | DOI: 10.1177/0306422020935800

MARTIN ROWSON
is a cartoonist for
The Guardian and
the author of various
books, including
The Communist
Manifesto (2018), a
graphic novel adap-
tion of the famous
19th century book

Less than social media

El Salvador's young president uses Twitter to crush freedom, and Covid-19 has made his work easier, writes **Stefano Pozzebon**

49(02): 48/49 | DOI: 10.1177/0306422020935801

WHEN NAYIB BUKELE took over as president of El Salvador in June 2019, the international community looked at the young leader with a mix of hope and excitement. Then the youngest head of state in the western hemisphere, it seemed the 37-year-old Bukele could usher in a new era for the troubled Central American nation – an era when El Salvador could finally leave behind the ghosts of the civil war that ended in 1992 and the criminal violence that followed it.

A year on, much of that excitement has faded and El Salvador seems resigned to deal yet again with a strongman in power (a *caudillo*) in the best Latin American tradition.

Make no mistake, Bukele still enjoys the support of the vast majority of his countrymen, who see in him something completely different from the discredited political leadership which ruled the country since the end of the war.

But behind the applause, journalists and human rights activists are sounding the alarm.

"I am the victim of a real hate campaign," said Nelson Rauda, a reporter at investigative portal El Faro, based in San Salvador. Rauda says that while covering a press conference in the presidential palace, Bukele first disputed his questions, then mocked him in public. After the press conference, one of the president's supporters created a meme of him bullying the journalist. After Bukele retweeted it, Rauda started receiving hundreds of hate messages on Twitter and other social media. The journalist says two fake accounts using his name were created to discredit him, and members of his family have been verbally attacked.

While the campaign never escalated to physical violence, Rauda's is far from the only example of such behaviour.

"This tells you about the atmosphere here," Rauda told Index. "There are so many cases [of online abuse]. At El Faro we showed how a former official account related to Bukele's campaign has evolved into a real trolling account used to smear and attack his opponents."

Like many other macho leaders around the world, Bukele is all over Twitter. He has an audience of two million followers (El Salvador has a population of 6.5 million) and often launches official policies through social media.

"I think he's the only president in the world that doesn't show his face to explain his policies. He just tweets," said Juan Carlos Quintero, a Salvadoran freelance photographer.

One episode is particularly indicative. On a Friday night during the coronavirus outbreak, a video showing people going out and about in La Libertad, a harbour city on the Pacific coast, went viral on social media. Seeing the video, Bukele tweeted that the city was under a total lockdown, and instructed the defence minister to enforce the new measure. The minister responded "as you order" in another tweet, and armoured vehicles started rolling into La Libertad. Only the following day did the government formally announce the measure.

Latin America has produced a variety of colourful leaders, but none of them has embraced social media the way Bukele has. He has been compared to a military dictator from the 1970s, but Bukele also seems to be from the future.

"He's the *caudillo* 2.0 – like the old ones, but with the software updated," said Rauda.

The coronavirus crisis has only cemented Bukele's grip on power. El Salvador was one of the first countries in the Americas to enforce a quarantine, even before any cases were registered.

While countries in Europe and America were scrambling with how to confront the virus, the Salvadoran president seemed to know what to do.

OPPOSITE: President Nayib Bukele at a news conference during quarantine, May 2020

From his Twitter account, Bukele made sure everyone knew the risks that came if they broke social distancing measures: Salvadorans who were found out of their homes without a valid reason could be detained for up to 30 days.

In a televised address in May, he asked his fellow citizens to close their eyes and "think of your dearest person in the world choking outside a hospital, without care", to paint a picture of the havoc the virus could wreak. Plenty of tweets followed, praising how powerful the image was, which were duly retweeted by the presidential account.

Bukele, whose New Ideas party was formed less than two years ago, now has his eyes firmly fixed on his next prize: the legislative elections to be held in February 2021. Despite his popularity, the president commands only a handful of seats in congress, which is still controlled by

He's the caudillo 2.0 – like the old ones, but with the software update

the traditional parties of the old guard.

Tiziano Breda, a political analyst based in Central America, has little doubt that things are going to change if the president wins a majority in the legislative. "Everything he's done so far has been a constant election campaign," he said. "What could happen next is really hard to predict." ⊗

Stefano Pozzebon *is a freelance journalist who writes from Latin America*

Nowhere left to hide?

The Turkey government has been attacking privacy for years now. Could the battle to control coronavirus eradicate what is left, asks **Kaya Genç**

49(02): 50/52 I DOI: 10.1177/0306422020935802

IN TURKEY, THE government strictly polices public life and privacy has become like an oasis in a desert. Since 2016, the Turkish state has expelled hundreds of thousands of public servants and arrested and imprisoned scores of academics and journalists. When people have spoken out against these measures, through public petitions and social media posts, it has cost thousands of private-sector workers their livelihoods. But in the privacy of their homes, at least, Turks have been able to speak their minds, hoping they are not being snooped on.

Now, as surveillance becomes a public-health tactic to tackle Covid-19, Turks face a conundrum: can they trust an autocratic state which may save their lives via contact-tracing not to come after them later for political reasons? In fighting Covid-19, could Turks give away what little they have left of their privacy?

President Recep Tayyip Erdogan rules by decree. Whatever he says goes. And he's made no secret of his plans to exploit the current situation. When he asked citizens to use the Life Fits Home app, developed by Turkey's Information and Communication Technologies Authority, it was a rhetorical question.

"Life Fits Home lets patients monitor their recovery; it also allows us to monitor their movements," health minister Fahrettin Koca said in April.

When Covid-19-infected users venture out, the app reminds them to self-isolate at home. It then notifies the closest police officer on duty.

The tracker's statistics detail infection rates, but its wealth of geolocation data could also help authorities to pursue citizens.

"Turkey won't only get rid of this coronavirus; it will also get rid of its media viruses and political viruses, God willing!" Erdogan declared in April, accusing journalists of spreading fake news.

"Life Fits Home is open to misuse," Kerem Altıparmak, the head of the Human Rights Centre of the Ankara Bar Association, told Index.

"We can't foresee how the app's data will be used, or by whom; there is no information about how to file a complaint in cases of privacy violation. People will use it on a voluntary basis, the minister says, but most will download it out of health concerns, not by free will."

Altıparmak is worried that the government could use Life Fits Home to limit personal freedom.

"The app requires a Turkish ID number for registration; it will know who you are and where you are, among other things," Yaman Akdeniz, a law professor at Istanbul Bilgi University, told Index.

"It's not clear whether it'll be used for ulterior purposes. This kind of data collection is a sensitive issue and could be misused by authorities.

"The fight against the Covid-19 pandemic should not be used as an opportunity to develop and use intrusive technologies on citizens."

Privacy and data protection are major concerns in Turkey.

The CEOs of communications companies Turk Telekom and Turkcell are both pro-Erdogan, often parroting his line on "national and native technology" and supporting his policies in pro-Erdogan newspapers.

During the 2016 coup attempt, Turkcell, the country's biggest mobile phone operator, disseminated the government's "take over the streets" texts to millions.

But foreign tech companies who hold the lion's share of Turks' private data

RIGHT: A woman receives a free food parcel at her home. People over 65 are banned from leaving their homes as part of Covid-19 restrictions

We're living in extraordinary times, but extraordinary times are the real test for government's respect [for] human rights

aren't as easy to tame. In April, the government drafted a law demanding Facebook, which owns WhatsApp, to store its Turkey-based users' data inside the country, allowing authorities access in case they required it.

The proposed law led to panicked WhatsApp conversations, and users deleted chat histories, fearing the government would word-search their conversations and prosecute them.

Not able to convince the public, the government withdrew the draft amendments. Akdeniz led the charge against this proposed law.

"It's a constant challenge to defend fundamental rights in Turkey," he said. "After the Covid-19 pandemic ends, Turkey has the potential to become more authoritarian – more people will be prosecuted for their criticism of the government."

Speed, in his view, should be the focus of privacy advocates. When he and lawyer Altıparmak challenged the government's Wikipedia ban at the Constitutional Court, it took 30 months before they could successfully reverse it.

Akdeniz worries that privacy campaigners will fail to catch up with the government's pace and be unable to challenge its intrusive new technologies quickly enough in courts.

"It'll take years to successfully challenge violations of privacy," he said.

As Turkey steers away from the west, allying with China, Russia and Venezuela, public pronouncements of allegiance to the governing party and its leader have become widespread.

Turkey is a deeply divided country: around half of the country supported Erdogan in the latest presidential election, and public sector employees in the other half of the population must hide their discontent to retain their jobs. Privately, they may not much care for →

Turkey won't only get rid of this coronavirus; it will also get rid of its media viruses and political viruses, God willing!

→ Erdogan and his loyalist wingmen, but they still have to sing their praises in public.

As Orhan Pamuk, Turkey's Nobel laureate, wrote, "the gulf between the private and public views of our countrymen is evidence of the power of the state".

Planned invasions into privacy may close this gulf and tilt the delicate balance.

Nate Schenkkan, the director for special research at Freedom House, acknowledges dangers concerning the privacy of ordinary Turkish citizens, but he is more worried about implications for dissidents, for whom violations of privacy have long been a major concern.

"The indictment of Osman Kavala, a rights defender and philanthropist imprisoned since 2017, is very much based on transcripts of his phone conversations recorded by law enforcement or Turkish intelligence," he told Index. "They've also amassed his texts and WhatsApp messages. Other surveillance measures included secret photographs of him taken during meetings in public places, sometimes obtained via hidden cameras."

This intrusion into Kavala's privacy, Schenkkan believes, was purposefully planned to create an "enormous chilling effect" on all activists in Turkey.

"You have to be mindful that Kavala's actions were extremely legal: organising training; applying for grants; emailing people about capacity building. After he was prosecuted, and others in his circle went into exile, there was a chilling effect in terms of how Turkish activists conducted their conversations."

Over the last eight years, Schenkkan has noticed a shift in how Turkish activists talk to him in private settings.

"In even fairly private conversations they pay increased attention to ensuring the privacy of our communications," he said.

"They move to different locations while talking, for example. I noticed some paranoid acts of caution that are not unjustified. When you learn that your fellow activists were under surveillance, and that their conversations were recorded, that changes the way you behave over time. If you're a journalist, you may change the subject you report on. If you're a researcher, you may change your research topic."

Tarık Beyhan, a director at Amnesty Turkey, told Index he was concerned that the state could use Covid-19 to "normalise technologies threatening our privacy rights".

He's hoping the pandemic does not give a green light to expand digital surveillance. "We're living in extraordinary times, but extraordinary times are the real test for government's respect [for] human rights," he said.

"Increased digital surveillance powers, like obtaining access to mobile phone location data, threatens privacy, freedom of expression and freedom of association. They also pose a risk of harm to dissidents. Since 2016's coup attempt, the government had been reluctant to relinquish its temporary powers. We mustn't sleepwalk into a permanent expanded surveillance state now."

For now, at least, we maintain some privacy and, as a result, Turks continue to debate and criticise government policies in private conversations.

"That is one of the most interesting things about the current privacy crisis," Schenkkan said. "People don't stop sharing their views. Some change their behaviour, but not everyone. There is a kind of resilience."

And some, of course, have been amassing great skills at how to carve out as much privacy as possible away from an interfering state – skills that might be more useful than ever in the coming months. ⊗

Kaya Genç *is the Turkish contributing editor to Index, based in Istanbul*

Open book?

Somak Ghoshal reports on fears that the Indian government could use a new Covid-19 tracing app to track journalists' contacts and movements

49(02): 53/55 I DOI: 10.1177/0306422020935803

INDEPENDENT INDIAN JOURNALISTS searching for an accurate story have to overcome many obstacles, and the challenges are likely only to increase in the coming months.

With the new Aarogya Setu smartphone app, which was launched in April to track Covid-19 infections, concerns have been raised that the government has a ready and easy tool to track allegiances – especially the contacts journalists cultivate.

With the lack of data security laws to protect citizens, is this public health surveillance mechanism going to be the death of privacy in India?

"We cannot yet say that Aarogya Setu will mark the end of the private space in India. But it certainly possesses the potential to bring about such an end," said Chennai-based lawyer Suhrith Parthasarathy.

The app is already the new normal for private and public sector employees. Many of them must download it to gain access to their workplaces, and in some cases to get paid.

In the future, citizens may need to have the go-ahead from the app, based on their health status, before they use public transport or take trains or flights.

The conflict between the public and the private is a crucial theme in India's democracy and is most apparent in the covert surveillance tactics the government has used since it came to power in 2014.

The biometric data-based universal identification number – the Aadhaar – allotted to every citizen is a point of contention, with its repeated leaks of private individual data.

"Combined with [the] Aadhaar and other tools that can enable surveillance (access to spending patterns through credit cards or electronic banking data), the state gets access to enormous information about an individual, making private conversations nearly impossible," said New York-based journalist and human-rights lobbyist Salil Tripathi.

Early in April, when the government launched the app and urged its 1.3 billion citizens to download it, its intention seemed legitimate.

Like the contact-tracing apps introduced by countries such as China, Norway and Singapore, Aarogya Setu aims to play a pivotal role in stemming the spread of Covid-19.

Based on Bluetooth connectivity and access to the GPS data of the user, the app records a person's whereabouts and health status. In doing so, it makes it possible for the government to track travel history, check contact with others and keep tabs on high-risk zones.

At the time of writing in mid May, India has close to 91,000 active cases of Covid-19, with more than 2,800 deaths. The country was in lockdown for weeks, leaving the economy badly shaken. With people desperate to get back to work, Aarogya Setu has been downloaded more than 100 million times already.

The pandemic has forced these new realities on the world, and there are concerns.

"What is worrisome is the mission, or scope, creep that may happen with measures taken by governments to protect their respective populations," said Mishi Choudhary, tech lawyer and founder of the New Delhi-based Software Freedom Law Centre. "Questions of privacy and security are not the top-of-mind concerns when a population is reeling from a deadly disease [and] economic and personal hardships."

In a recent article in The Hindu, Parthasarathy, along with lawyers Gautam Bhatia and Apar Gupta, confirmed suspicions that the app did not meet "minimum legal requirements".

It warned: "Any temporary measures [governments] impose have a disturbing habit of entrenching themselves into the landscape and creating a 'new normal' well after the crisis has passed."

Parthasarathy told Index: "In India, we do not yet have a data protection law. The

→ makers of Aarogya Setu claim there are solid data protection principles that undergird the application. But in the absence of legislation, this doesn't even 'give an appearance of solidity to pure wind', to borrow [George] Orwell's words."

Days after we spoke to Parthasarathy, French "ethical hacker" Robert Baptiste – who goes by the pseudonym Elliot Alderson on Twitter – exposed security breaches in the app.

On 10 May, he tweeted screenshots of records of people quarantined in the central Indian state of Madhya Pradesh. The dashboard of the app revealed their names (blacked out by Baptiste), the devices they used, details of their operating systems and the GPS coordinates of their current locations and those of their offices. "This is what a surveillance system looks like," he said.

Contact-tracing apps can be useful and legitimate tools to safeguard public health, if used with checks and balances.

The National Health Service in the UK, for instance, has published the open source code of its contact-tracing app.

Not only does India lack such transparency but the government's instruction to manufacturers to pre-install the app on all new smartphones by default amounts to coercion and overreach of power.

Before the government led by Narendra Modi came to power in 2014, riding on a wave of militant Hindu nationalism, India's last brutal brush with state surveillance was under the reign of Indian National Congress leader Indira Gandhi.

In 1975, the then prime minister imposed a state of emergency, suspending the fundamental rights of citizens and curbing freedom of press.

Modi's rule, now in its second term, harks back to those dark days. From the arrest and indefinite detention of human-rights activists such as Sudha Bharadwaj, Gautam Navlakha and Anand Teltumbde, without trial and under a draconian anti-terrorist law, to a series of attacks on journalists for reporting unpleasant truths, the government has relentlessly stifled dissent in its six years in power.

Ironically, a section of the corporate media, operating with the financial blessings of the political class, continues to back it. They were the cheerleaders for the revocation of the special constitutional privileges of Jammu and Kashmir last year, followed by the imposition of one of the longest communication curbs in the region.

Be it his overnight decision to demonetise high-value currency notes in 2016 that sent the economy into a tailspin or his government's neglect of the horrific plight of migrant workers during the lockdown, Modi can do no wrong in the eyes of these media allies.

Unsurprisingly, the government's retaliation against independent journalists who are exposing the human costs of the pandemic is severe. Siddharth Varadarajan, founding editor of news platform The Wire, was recently summoned by police to Ayodhya, a city in Uttar Pradesh, 435 miles away from his home in Delhi, during the height of the national lockdown, when travel even within cities was severely restricted.

The government's instruction to manufacturers to pre-install the app on all new smartphones by default amounts to coercion

By reporting a story on the chief minister of Uttar Pradesh – a firebrand Hindu priest appointed by Modi called Yogi Adityanath – violating physical distancing norms as he attended a gathering at a temple, The Wire incurred the wrath of pro-Modi officials.

The Adityanath government has repeatedly lashed out against journalists who show the regime in an unfavourable light. After a local newspaper reported that the lockdown had forced starving children in Varanasi – Modi's electoral constituency – to eat grass, authorities threatened to take legal action unless an apology was offered.

As well as the media, members of the medical community are also likely to face hardships.

Already facing attacks from the public, evicted by landlords and ostracised by neighbours as potential carriers of the virus, they are going to be easily identified by an app such as Aarogya Setu. If their information gets leaked, it may prove detrimental to their safety rather than protecting them.

"This app is only an extension of capabilities the private sector has deployed," said Gayathri Vaidyanathan, an independent Delhi-based journalist. "The issue is that private companies have already normalised surveillance, and today we are happy to part with our data and privacy in exchange for coupons and vouchers.

"The government is now deploying surveillance, and the danger is that this will become the new normal. We will grow accustomed to Big Brother watching us in exchange for 'greater security'." ⊗

Somak Ghoshal *is a journalist based in Bengaluru, India*

MAIN: Graffiti of
Viktor Orbán with the
word obey on a wall
in Budapest

IN FOCUS

Knife-edge politics

Ahead of the Serbian election, **Marina Lalovic** interviews **Ana Lalic**, the journalist whose arrest prompted the government to rethink what could be reported in her country

49(02): 58/60 I DOI: 10.1177/0306422020935804

WHEN A STATE of emergency was introduced in Serbia on 15 March, it included rules restricting from whom journalists could source information on the virus to just the prime minister and a "crisis unit".

Two weeks later, when journalist Ana Lalic published a piece about the shortages of personal protective equipment in a hospital in the city of Novi Sad, contradicting the government line, she was arrested for "inciting panic and disturbing public opinion".

Index caught up with her to find out what happened next, and what her worries are about the state of journalism today.

Lalic, a magazine journalist for Nova.rs, said that on the day of publication, "at around 10pm six policemen showed up on my doorstep with the search warrant". She added: "Before they came in, I managed to send to my newsroom our response to the hospital's denial, which was published while I was being arrested. They took my mobile phone and laptop. After I gave my statement to the police, the prosecutor ordered, by phone, 48 hours' arrest. They took me to prison where I spent the night sitting on a bed next to which was a toilet behind a couple of dirty blankets. At 9am the next day, the police took me to the prosecutor where I presented my defence and denied all the charges. They let me go but they didn't drop the charges. I had to defend myself outside the prison."

The problem, according to Lalic, who is a board member of the Independent Journalists' Association of Vojvodina, was that "I contradicted everything that the Serbian government wanted to present as a truth: that the country was absolutely prepared for the pandemic, that we had the best health system in Europe and that, with regards to medical equipment, we had more than we need".

In reality, she added, Serbian hospitals have been falling apart in the last 30 years and doctors are emigrating because of the catastrophic working conditions. At the beginning of the epidemic, for two weeks it was impossible to get masks, gloves or disinfectant gel in any of the pharmacies. "By arresting me they wanted to hide the real situation. But they triggered the opposite reaction: many health workers started to confirm that they worked with the minimum of protective equipment. They've been provided with one mask and one pair of gloves on a daily basis while treating tens of patients."

The health institutions, according to internal information, banned all employees from talking to the media, at risk of being fired. Unofficial sources were the only way to get to the truth.

RIGHT: Serbian reporter Ana Lalic, who was arrested in March for reporting on shortages of protective gear at hospitals

Right after your arrest, the government restriction on information during the pandemic was withdrawn. Why do you think this happened?
Charges against me were withdrawn after three weeks because the prosecutor decided that there was not reasonable suspicion for further prosecution. The government's →

They took me to prison where I spent the night sitting on a bed next to which was a toilet behind a couple of dirty blankets

Many health workers started to confirm that they worked with the minimum of protective equipment

→ measure on media censorship was withdrawn the day after my arrest because of the pressure coming from public opinion across the whole region. Many European officials and EU institutions on media freedom came to know about my arrest, so I soon became really bad news for the regime of the president, Aleksandar Vučić.

You have 20 years' experience. How does this time compare with the attitudes to the media during the Balkan Wars, and recently?
The independent media in Serbia have been constantly targeted over the last eight years, during the time that Vučić has been in power. He was previously minister of information during the [Yugoslav leader] Slobodan Milošević regime. While Vučić was minister of information, from 1998 to 2000, he implemented an information law under which journalists were sanctioned with enormous fines if they were critical of the Milošević regime.

We are called traitors and foreign spies on a daily basis. We've been accused of working against Serbia. This attitude towards journalists is a reason why we've been receiving negative reactions and threats on the streets from citizens as well. Government representatives refuse to answer our questions containing any critical points.

How has your work changed since the beginning of the pandemic?
While I'm answering your questions, in front of my house there are security guards provided by my magazine. Every time I leave my house, I carry a panic taser. On the same day I received a Deutsche Welle award for reporting during the pandemic, somebody cut my car tyres. Apart from centralised and prepared information that the government and the crisis centre are providing, it's impossible to get to the official sources. That's why the journalist's job during the pandemic in Serbia is almost impossible if you are not part of the regime media that publishes only everything that government wants you to. If you try to be a journalist, you risk what I just experienced.

What is the current situation regarding reporting on Covid-19?
On 7 May, the state of emergency ended, so reporting is supposed to continue as before the pandemic. But this won't bring a huge change in our work, because the division between the pro-regime media and those who are not has never been greater. In Serbia we are moving towards our next electoral campaign for the parliamentary elections, due to be held on 21 June. This could hold new dangers: media freedom will become more restricted, and there will be a massive propaganda push by the government.

Is it legitimate to compare the current state of the media in Serbia to the 1990s?
It's unbelievable but, increasingly, independent journalists will tell you that we haven't experienced such conditions before – not even during the Milošević regime [during the Balkan Wars]. Even under this wartime regime there was more media freedom, and more media were reporting objectively and professionally. Pro-regime tabloids today are leading a campaign not just against political opposition parties but also against their colleagues that work in the independent media. This didn't come even to Milošević's mind. ⊗

Marina Lalovic is a Serbian journalist, based in Rome, working for Radio Rai 3 and Radio3 Mondo

Stage right (and wrong)

Playwright **David Hare** tells **Jemimah Steinfeld** about why plays must challenge group-think, government propaganda and his new poem, which is published here for the first time

49(02): 61/63 I DOI: 10.1177/0306422020935805

FOR DAVID HARE, too many plays right now "are restatements of the bleeding obvious". There's a problem in contemporary British theatre: we've all become a little bit too nice, trapped in a mentality that says the arts must affirm popular narratives and must never offend.

"I go to an awful lot of plays where I am told that racism is a bad thing or sexism is a bad thing or that gender is fluid or that gay people are as entitled to love as heterosexual people... Platitudes of the day are rehearsed and we leave the theatre and we feel confirmed," the award-winning playwright told Index.

Hare, who wrote the plays Skylight and Plenty, believes this "herd-mindedness" is distinctly new to the 21st century. Twentieth-century playwrights, by contrast, "saw themselves as rebels against common wisdom rather than just confirming the common wisdom".

"The playwright, in my view, has always been the person who is out ahead of public pace and so the great plays of the 20th century – which would include Waiting for Godot or Look Back in Anger – are outstandingly ugly and almost incomprehensible when they first appear. People go, 'Oh my goodness, what is this? I don't know what this is'."

The desire to avoid offence doesn't extend just to plays. It concerns the personal profile of playwrights too, he argues.

"In the current atmosphere, someone like Strindberg is completely unperformable because the consensus is he's a misogynist... You reach the point where you say, 'Is there absolutely nothing that Strindberg can tell us at all?'."

It's a pertinent question, especially for someone such as Hare. While his career has seen his name on screenplays including Oscar-winning film The Hours, the bread-and-butter of his writing has been plays that poke fun at the British political establishment.

Hare willingly admits he's spent his "whole life giving offence" and says it's a basic right that he defends very strongly.

He believes you cannot be a writer "and not be 100% in favour of free speech".

Hare senses he is not alone in being frustrated by the current creative output. He references the popular US television series Succession which satirises the upper echelons of New York society. He says people "fall on it with gratitude precisely because it doesn't express the common view of what's going on but treats these people as intrinsically ridiculous".

Hare is also "driven absolutely mad" by the idea that a writer's literary influence comes from the writings of others. For Hare "it's to do with the life you've lived and what you see around you and the world."

It was with this thought in mind that he penned the poem Influence, which is published here for the first time.

Hare, who has been writing poetry for about six years, describes himself as "a nervous poet", an amateur of sorts – something which can, on a level, act as a strength.

"I'm working as a poet completely outside knowledge of what is going on in the world of poetry and that gives me a wonderful freedom actually to know absolutely nothing about the state of contemporary poetry," he said. →

Platitudes of the day are rehearsed, and we leave the theatre and we feel confirmed

ABOVE: Award-winning playwright David Hare in Allen Ginsberg's study

a particular kind of patrician who interfered all the time with what dramas were saying".

It's a damning statement from a man whose play Fanshen, about communism in China, was subjected to more than 110 requests for changes to the text. But Hare believes that kind of very crude political censorship is not how the BBC works anymore, and actually singles out the organisation for praise.

"It's one of the few hosts to all differing points of view, far more than any of the newspapers that criticise the BBC all the time – the BBC actually welcomes all points of view and that's why it is the single most important element in the contract of free speech in Great Britain," he said.

The BBC's free speech record might be on the up, the government's less so.

A few days before speaking to Index, Hare had been interviewed by BBC Radio 4 about the government's handling of the coronavirus.

Hare, who had been ill with the virus himself, chastised the government for not being truthful to the population.

He tells Index that the first film he ever made, Licking Hitler, was about a British propaganda unit during World War II.

"This is very, very dirty stuff," he said, explaining that public units which lie have always been part of government apparatus, before going on to say that "it feels as if that unit is now running the government".

Hare, born in 1947, believes people in the

→   And what if people cite him as an influence?

"If I give people fortitude or comfort or if, by what I do or say, I give them the courage to do what they want to do and to say, then I'm terribly proud of that and any writer who says to me 'It's your example I admire', great," he said.

"But when they start saying 'I'm trying to do what you do', then I do get extremely jumpy and, by and large, I don't think that the plays that are 'influenced' by me are very good."

Hare's outspoken attitude has prompted criticism over the years. The journalist Bernard Levin once wrote that he wished "David Hare would go away". It's with the BBC, though, that Hare has had the most problems when it comes to free speech.

It was "the most censorious organisation that I have had to work with", he said, "particularly in the 1970s when it was just run by

UK are "being as badly governed as at any stage in my lifetime".

He does not see the government as having the same authoritarian tendencies as seen in countries such as Jair Bolsonaro's Brazil and Viktor Orbán's Hungary – the latter of which he describes as a "lying machine" – but asks why, in a social democracy, truth would "not be your best friend"?.

That question of truth has been central to much of Hare's writing. Take the screenplay Denial, about the trial of Deborah Lipstadt brought by Holocaust-denier David Irving.

"Denial is about something which is so unbelievably important. You know – how do we now fight the counter-myth that is growing, particularly now that, obviously, the

The playwright, in my view, has always been the person who is out ahead of public pace

generation who grew up who experienced the camps are dying?

"How does the truth defend itself and how does the truth fight?" ⊗

Jemimah Steinfeld is the deputy editor of Index on Censorship

INFLUENCE

by DAVID HARE

FOR G.B.

"Who are your influences?" the interviewer asks, as though
There were the foggiest chance that I might know.
I long ago mastered the rudiments of the game
But surely no two players then play the same?

Drop-shot, lob, forehand, backhand, second service, smash,
Patrol the base-line, define your territory before you do anything rash
The rhythms of control become unconscious after a while
Yes, you can learn technique, but how can anyone teach you style?

"Surely you admire someone special?" the interviewer says
But no good player expects to play exactly how Federer plays.
They can't. Of course I like Chekhov, Ibsen, O'Casey, O'Neill.
They're great. But, sorry, it's a given, I can't feel how they feel.

Nor would I wish to. I don't work in their slipstream. It's clear
A playwright can't hear dialogue with a borrowed ear
The purpose is not to emulate another woman or man
The purpose is to write as well as you possibly can.

And only you. That's the point. Why else would I bother
To write my play if I meant its fate to be to echo another?
Feeling desperate, feeling hopeless, I can only repeat
"What are your influences?" "People, history, the street."

David Hare is an award-winning playwright and filmmaker. He has written over thirty stage plays which include Plenty, Pravda (with Howard Brenton) and Skylight, and screenplays including The Hours and Denial

Inside story: Hungary's media silence

Viktória Serdült reports on a new era of journalism where people are warned not to speak to reporters

49(02): 64/66 | DOI: 10.1177/0306422020935806

UNDER THE GLASS roof of the lobby of the prime minister's cabinet office, journalists gathered from all over Budapest to listen to the daily press conference of the operational corps, responsible for defence efforts against the coronavirus. It was mid-March and tensions were already running high: just a week earlier, Prime Minister Viktor Orbán had announced the first confirmed cases, and the country was just hours away from the declaration of a national emergency.

The journalists had probing, critical questions. Why were people with a fever sent home from hospitals without testing? Why didn't the authorities test people with obvious symptoms? Was it a coincidence that the first cases were blamed on young Iranian students when rumours were circulating of elderly people with pneumonia in hospitals already in February?

But the unexpected came when a reporter from Hungary's biggest TV channel, RTL Klub, took her turn: a press officer grabbed the microphone out of her hands while she was asking her question.

"We both have other things to do," the police representative on the podium told her.

A few days later, at a similar press conference, one of Orbán's press officers went even further when asked about testing protocols.

"You shouldn't be smarter than epidemiological experts," he warned journalists.

Several months have since passed, and the lobby of the ministry is empty. Worse still, attacks on journalists have escalated to such an extent that many fear we are now beyond the point where media critical of the government can easily exist.

Press conferences called by the operational corps about the virus are held in a TV studio. Questions from journalists must be submitted by email two hours beforehand, and they have no comeback on the answers. Press officers examine them and make a careful selection: critical questions are often ignored, and those that are not ignored are usually given blunt and uninformative answers.

Journalists at the few independent papers that remain in the country are used to being ignored by authorities under Orbán's rule. Emails sent to ministries are left unanswered, and phone numbers for press offices are never direct lines – some have even deleted the numbers from their websites. Sources are harder to get; even when they speak, they do so anonymously for fear of retaliation.

"I respect your work and I know I promised to help, but someone from the ministry told me it would be unwise to speak to you," was the answer I got from a healthcare professional on the phone recently.

Even under such circumstances, the remnants of the independent media manage to publish stories of corruption, political intrigue and affairs of the state. But in the wake of the global pandemic, the strict rules have drastically changed for the worse. Some now fear there may be long-term effects from which independent media will never recover.

On 30 March, parliament – with its two-thirds government majority – passed the Coronavirus Act. This gives Orbán the right to rule by decree for an indefinite time (though he has since announced that he will return the special

powers by end of May). It also introduced jail terms of up to five years for intentionally spreading misinformation that hinders the government response to the pandemic. What "intentionally spreading misinformation" means is not specified.

Newsrooms all over the country quickly responded by compiling legal guidelines for their staff, and journalists started checking their information not twice but three or four times before handing their stories to editors. Around 107 cases were filed for spreading misinformation during the state of emergency, by the time this magazine went to press. The news programme of M1 state television has also launched a series called "Debunking fake news" in which it only portrays articles from independent media, with no opportunity to defend themselves.

I spoke to a doctor who warned me not to write down what I heard because they would be fired

The Hungarian Civil Liberties Union, an NGO, published a report after speaking to many independent newsrooms about their experiences since the pandemic started. Many complained of centralised communication, not having access to information and the unwillingness of their sources to speak out.

One of the journalists interviewed said: "I spoke to a doctor who warned me not to write down what I heard because they would be fired, and I would be sent to jail."

Ten years ago, it would have been unimaginable for state propaganda to call journalists liars

→ Another journalist compared the control over the media to a giant snake: "Every time we breathe, it tightens its grip even more."

Szabolcs Panyi, an investigative journalist at Direkt36, speaks of similar experiences.

"It has been a long tradition of the Hungarian government to ignore or refuse media inquiries [and] interview or FOI requests by independent journalists. However, the Covid-19 situation triggered further centralisation and restrictions in government communications. For example, a topic my outlet tries to cover is the price, quality and certifications of the protective equipment and Covid-19 tests the Hungarian government procures from China. This should be public information as they are bought [with] taxpayers' money, but we know very little about these purchases," he told Index.

The biggest fear of independent journalists is that the snake will never let them go. Many agree that the growing control and centralisation of state communication will have long-lasting consequences when the pandemic is over.

Being familiar with the media policy of the Orbán government, Ágnes Urbán, an analyst at Mérték Media Monitor, also finds it hard to believe that things will return to the way they were before the emergency.

"It is obvious that the government exploits the pandemic to centralise its power even more, confine publicity and eliminate the still-existing elements of checks and balances – not to mention that publishers need to face unprecedented economic challenges," she said.

Zsombor György is no stranger to the government's attacks. After the original Magyar Nemzet was shut down, where he used to work, he and his colleagues founded Magyar Hang, an independent weekly. Their paper has been under attack ever since and was among the first to be labelled "fake news" in the new state television series. Though some may think otherwise, he believes the only option is to fight back against accusations, so Magyar Hang filed an official complaint to the Media Council, Hungary's most powerful media regulatory body.

"If society is made to believe we tell lies, there is a huge problem. When state TV says you are spreading fake news, it is our duty to fight back," he told Index.

Editor-in-chief György thinks Hungarian society lacks media literacy, meaning people fail to understand that publicity is power and can have consequences.

"The old way of reporting from the countryside was to speak to the school principal, the mayor, the innkeeper and the parish priest. Now they either do not have the authority to speak or are afraid to do so. Important stories never reach the public as a result," he added.

But it is not only ordinary people who are reluctant to speak out. György thinks there is growing fear among critical journalists as well, which may lead to self-censorship. In the meantime, government attacks against the free press are so frequent people are ceasing to even notice them.

"Ten years ago, it would have been unimaginable for state propaganda to call journalists liars. Now the narrative against independent media runs through propaganda outlets one by one. On pro-government news channel Hír TV there are programmes where commentators discuss police actions against them. By the time this happens in real life, ordinary people will not be surprised," he said.

Even if society may be prepared for such things to happen, the idea remains terrifying for independent journalists.

"They are already afraid, so Orbán will never need black cars in the middle of the night to take reporters away," György said. "He knows very well what he is doing." ⊗

Viktória Serdült is a Hungarian journalist, who works for hvg.hu, one of the few independent news sites in Hungary

Life under lockdown: A Kashmiri journalist

Index talks to **Bilal Hussain**, a journalist in Kashmir, about the impact of India's internet shutdown on the region, his life and his work

49(02): 67/67 | DOI: 10.1177/0306422020935807

Tell us about yourself
I was the business editor for local dailies that include Greater Kashmir and Kashmir Times. I live in Srinagar, the summer capital city of Jammu and Kashmir, with my family.

Has the coronavirus lockdown left people feeling even more isolated?
I have witnessed people crying when they could finally speak to loved ones after months of no communication. This has taken a heavy toll on people's mental health.

How does the internet shutdown affect your day-to-day life?
Like other journalists, I was forced to use the internet at a government-run "media facilitation centre" for months ... on the computers installed by the state, thereby compromising internet security and privacy.

There was no privacy at all. Even fellow journalists could look through [my] emails.

I had to create a new email ID to use on government-installed computers to communicate with my editors, so that the authorities would not have access to our past conversations.

Are people using creative ways to subvert the shutdown?

Since March 2020, the government allowed restricted internet access that blocked many news websites. So journalists installed VPNs that could break the firewall and enabled journalists to access those websites.

Some journalists used to travel to Delhi to access the internet and came back after filing their reports.

To get video interviews to my editor in Paris, I put them on a memory stick and gave it to a friend who was travelling to the USA, and he sent it on from there.

What challenges are you facing with work?
The abrogation of Article 370 in August 2019 was a historic story for my generation, and as a journalist I was not able to tell it to the world because of the internet blackout.

Even today, I frequently lose opportunities to report on the situation unfolding in Kashmir.

Do you feel free to write about the pandemic without persecution from the government?
My fellow journalists have been charged for writing social media posts. This was a message to journalists to stifle and not to deviate from the state narrative.

I tried to venture out in the initial days of lockdown to report on Covid-19. However, the Indian military didn't allow me to go more than 1km from my home, so I couldn't report.

Has the internet shutdown left people in Kashmir without access to critical information about the coronavirus pandemic?
The situation is so tragic here that even doctors were not able to download critical-care guidelines recommended by the World Health Organisation. ⊗

As told to **Orna Herr**

RIGHT: Kashmiri journalist Bilal Hussain, who continues to work despite the internet shutdown

The truth will out

More than ever, journalists must pursue the facts in these uncertain times, says **John Lloyd**

49(02): 68/70 I DOI: 10.1177/0306422020935808

JOURNALISTS OFTEN QUOTE the third president of the USA as writing that between "a government without newspapers and newspapers without a government, I should not hesitate a moment to prefer the latter".

As Thomas Jefferson came to realise, he needed to rethink. Only democratic governments – using the rule of law and with a free civil society – can guarantee the conditions for free media. The free media's responsibility in 2020 and for the future must be to seek for something like the truth, within the inevitable limits of time, space, libel law and audience attention.

Saying "something like" is to acknowledge that we cannot escape those limits – especially for complex investigations. But those challenges are incredibly important while, during this global crisis, the public works out who it can trust.

Bill Keller, former executive editor of The New York Times, told me that coverage of justice has "been a casualty of the economic trauma of our business". Keller, who also founded the Marshall Project, a website covering US criminal justice, said: "It's complicated, time-consuming investigative or quasi-investigative work; it's just something that most [media] organisations don't feel they can afford any longer."

A search for the facts which govern our lives has always meant holding every kind of power to account, to pose awkward questions, to provide space for dissident voices and to uncover secrets whose publication is in the public interest. And of course, this is of vital interest during the coronavirus pandemic.

This hasn't been stopped – though it has been diverted – by the loud contempt the 45th US president unceasingly shows for journalism. Donald Trump monopolises press conferences and uses them to harangue and insult those journalists who press him for hard facts on a pandemic, which is growing exponentially. He may rail, but the legal, political and civil institutions of the USA are, so far, strong enough to protect the space for combative journalism.

Steve Coll, director of the Columbia University Graduate School of Journalism, even gives his behaviour an optimistic spin. Trump's attacks, he says, have "really clarified what journalism is about... and why the founding fathers thought a really healthy press was important".

Other societies are not so lucky. The authoritarian rulers – China's Xi Jinping, Russia's Vladimir Putin, Egypt's Abdel Fattah el-Sisi, Turkey's Recep Tayyip Erdogan, Hungary's Viktor Orbán – all, as the US economist Joseph Stiglitz observes, "made sure when they came to power that the first thing they did was to close down the independent media".

Power, especially autocratic power, says Ezio Mauro, former editor of the Rome-based daily La Repubblica, "has an insuppressible temptation – the temptation of the balcony", referring to the speeches Mussolini would give from the balcony of the Palazzo Venezia in Rome.

"It is to transform the consensus acquired from one political sector – which is always temporary – into an everlasting totality, transforming the citizen into the public, the public into the people, and the people into an applauding crowd," he said.

CREDIT: Stellina Chen/Cartoon Movement

Where there's room for optimism is in the apparently unquenchable proactivity of journalists who are creating space for a journalism of fact and varied opinion.

Alexandra Vladimirova, a young journalist who has researched corruption in Russian sport, said: "For the Russian audience it is often not easy to understand who is who and who can be trusted. On the other hand, despite all the problems and prohibitions, there are still possibilities to do what you believe in."

India did have plenty of room for independent journalism but journalists are now being increasingly harried and threatened. For example, Siddharth Varadarajan, founder of news site The Wire, has been caught in a web of charges including creating panic and spreading rumours

The government condemns those journalists who try to tell the truth [as] anti-nationalist

designed to cause a riot – a group of alleged crimes which could attract a jail sentence of up to 20 years.

"Across India," Varadarajan wrote in The New York Times in April, "the pandemic and lockdown have provided an occasion for the free play of authoritarian impulses." The investigative journalist Rana Ayyub said that much of the coverage of the pandemic in India portrayed it as "a Muslim plague... and

We live in a world in which the means of manipulation have gone forth and multiplied

→   the government condemns those journalists who try to tell the truth [as] anti-nationalist".

Nothing in the democracies of Europe and North America, in Japan, Australia and New Zealand, approaches the level of suppression in the authoritarian states.

Instead, there are the challenges of freedom, of the market and of the relentless growth in power of the tech companies which are both destroying and gathering-in the functions of the news media. There is also the continued decline of newspapers – still the medium which employs most journalists.

"We have yet to craft a durable economic basis for a new era of journalistic independence in the digital age, free from government control and sustainable, whether commercially or through philanthropy," said Coll.

The few newspapers which remain economically healthy, and look like continuing to be so, include The New York Times, the Financial Times, The Economist and very few others.

We also see the constant intrusions of fake news. According to Peter Pomerantsev, who directs a programme on the burgeoning falsities of autocratic governments at the London School of Economics, "we live in a world in which the means of manipulation have gone forth and multiplied – a world of dark ads, psy-ops, hacks, bots, soft facts, deep fakes, fake news, Putin, trolls and Trump". The spread of fact-checking sites and centres helps, but much depends on the ability of citizens and institutions to sort the false from the true.

As Russia's army moved into Georgia in 2008, annexed the Ukrainian province of Crimea in 2014 and sponsored and reinforced the breakaway factions, it unleashed what the US-based Rand Corporation called "a firehose of falsehood", where visible interventions and reinforcements were flatly denied and labelled as western lies.

As the US scholar Martha Bayles has written, this "firehose" has the intent "to pollute the global information space with disinformation, conspiracy theories and paranoid fantasies in the hope of sowing division and cynicism among the citizens of liberal democracies".

We also see the widening division in our societies as another challenge for journalism. Citizens around the world, most clearly in Europe and the USA, have – through votes and demonstrations – signalled their radical alienation from politics, an alienation disproportionately concentrated in lower income groups. Part of this is due to being ignored by the news media, as much as by politicians and officials.

These protests should cause journalists to reflect on how the economic shocks of the past two decades have caused a series of crises. We must now examine where the coverage has been scanty or absent and how journalists, especially in "elite media", have accepted the dominant political and economic explanations, giving little space to those who see themselves as the victims.

Journalism will always depend on good democratic governments. Yet government and civil society depend on journalism remaining independent, accepting the responsibility of truth-telling, account-holding and attention-getting.

Independence means giving expression to differing, including unwelcome, opinions.

In a constantly shifting media space, where possibilities for free expression jostle with a narrowing of coverage and the cull of newspaper reporters, there's a tendency for the news media to huddle round one political pole.

Jochen Buchsteiner, a senior foreign correspondent for the Frankfurter Allgemeine Zeitung, in Germany, believes journalists must also let both sides be heard. "Activism, be it for a 'good cause', should be for others," he said. "Our task is to allow and understand complexity, reduce it and explain it in a fair manner. I don't see any other way to preserve – or win back – our credibility and value." ⊗

John Lloyd is an author and a contributing editor to the Financial Times

Extremists use virus to curb opposition

As Covid-19 spreads to Yemen and Iraq, there are fears that it will provide the perfect excuse for religious militia to further strangle free expression, writes **Laura Silvia Battaglia**

49(02): 71/73 I DOI: 10.1177/0306422020935809

NEWS THAT THE world was facing a global pandemic had only just been announced when militias in Yemen rushed through death sentences against journalists Abdulkhaleq Amran, Akram al-Waleedi, Hareth Hameed and Tawfiq al-Mansouri, after detaining them for five years.

The four journalists were charged with "spreading false news in support of the crimes of Saudi aggression and its allies against the Republic of Yemen".

At the same court proceedings, six other detained journalists were given "time-served" sentences and three years' probation. Unlike in the past, the lawyer Abdel Majeed Farea Sabra could do nothing for them:

"I was unable to properly represent my clients," he told Index. "They would not let me into the courtroom so I could not defend them. When the sentence was handed down, I wasn't allowed to appeal."

Militia in Yemen are using the distraction of Covid-19 to clean the country of "unsavoury" voices and push their religious agenda further. Part of that process involves downplaying the presence of Covid-19 in the country.

Online daily Al-Monitor reported that Mohammed Abdulqudoos, deputy director of Saba, North Yemen's official news agency, had tweeted that one case of Covid-19 – a woman coming from Saudi Arabia who was placed in isolation after testing positive – had been discovered in Sana'a, only to retract it a few hours later.

In a similar vein, a medical professional working with teams handling Covid-19 cases in Sana'a, who asked to remain anonymous, reported that four suspected coronavirus cases were identified in the first week of April. He said the patients were in isolation at the Movenpick Hotel in the city but that "these cases must remain a secret. If the Houthi find out that the news has leaked, there will be severe consequences".

The secrecy serves a very specific purpose. Abdulqudoos said: "They don't want the people, especially potential fighters, to be scared and distracted from the main cause, which is the war against the Saudis and their Yemeni government allies, which they are finally winning."

Even when the North Yemeni militias admitted their first coronavirus death in an announcement by health minister Taha al-Mutawakkil, the virus was still not presented as a risk.

Elisabeth Kendall, a senior research fellow at Pembroke College, Oxford, and an expert on the fragmented network of Islamist militias in Yemen, believes that the groups controlling the different parts of the country are using the pandemic to further their own causes. →

They don't want the people, especially potential fighters, to be scared and distracted from the main cause, which is the war against the Saudis and their Yemeni government allies

→ "The propaganda machine – fed by Yemen's Houthi at present, al-Qaeda affiliate Aqap remaining silent for now – is spreading the message that the virus was sent by Allah to punish the west and other enemies of Islam, like China.

"According to this narrative, the virus is an invisible soldier who would punish infidel societies, which are based on capitalism and globalisation, and whose governments have wasted money on fighting wars on Islam instead of investing in healthcare."

In this version of events, Islam is to be embraced because it is a hygienic religion and people should use the time in quarantine and lockdown as an essential time to learn more about Islam. Kendall said: "There is this imagery of humanity trapped in the dark, like the Koranic (and also Biblical) story of Jonah inside the whale. It looks like the time for an apocalyptic showdown is approaching."

Fatima Abo Alasar, a Yemeni scholar at the Middle East Institute in Washington DC, also believes that the situation is being used to extend the message of religious extremism.

"After years and years of war, it's very difficult to react to religious extremism and censorship, especially if these militia provide you [with] essentials that the government wasn't able to give you in years," she told Index. "I don't want to simplify the complexity, but people at the beginning accepted Houthis – like in Iraq they did with Islamic State – because they were able to provide electricity, heaters, jobs, fuel, in areas neglected by the government. This is the strategy of religious militias.

"Then, after everything settles down, they start the law enforcement, the censorship, the threats."

It's a similar situation in Iraq. In the province of Saladin, for example, around the city of Jurf al-Nasr, north of Babylon, the jihadist groups that survived the collapse of Isis are targeting Iraq-state sponsored Shia Hashd al-Shaabi militias, equivalent to ranks within the Iraqi military. Both sides have incurred deaths in the clashes.

The pandemic has been used here as a pretext to enforce greater control, including over the press. In Iraqi Kurdistan and Baghdad, a number of restrictive actions have been taken against the broadcaster NRT after it accused the authorities in Erbil of altering the number of Covid-19 infections and deaths to discourage the demonstrations that have been inflaming the country since summer 2019. Reuters has also clashed with the Baghdad government. Its licence was suspended when it published a story saying Covid-19 cases were not being correctly reported.

As in Yemen, the narrative that is often being pushed is firmly along religious lines.

Emma Sky, author of The Unravelling: High Hopes and Missed Opportunities in Iraq, said: "Muqtada al-Sadr [a Shia politician and cleric] and his militia blamed Trump for the spread of Covid-19 and said he will never accept any cure made by the infidels. Also, he blamed same-sex marriage for Covid-19."

Some mullahs are using the opportunity to fight secular tendencies amongst millennials, calling for people to observe Islamic prayers strictly. They're saying that if people do this, and perform the correct rituals around washing, Covid-19 will not arrive.

In Yemen, the fear and confusion are tangible when you talk to people on the street.

Aisha al-Jalal, a mother-of-seven from Atharish, a suburb on the outskirts of the capital, told Index: "Until now, we always thought no one could get it here because Yemen has been isolated for five years. They told us that all we had to do was wash our hands and wear masks, and also to drink infusions of lemon, ginger and

It looks like the time for an apocalyptic showdown is approaching

LEFT: A woman walking through the old town in Sanaa, Yemen

other herbs to protect ourselves. I make it for my children every day. Allah will save us."

She wouldn't say any more because of fears for her own safety.

But in Iraq, where there is more freedom from religion, street protests that began last year continue. Even amid the lockdown, daily demonstrations are staged in Baghdad's Tahrir Square. This might be in part because of Iraq's new prime minister, Mustafa al-Kadhimi, who took office in May.

"[He] maintains that Iraqis have the right to protest and he insists on the freedom of the media," said Sky.

"He himself has a background in civil society and was once a journalist. Now there are some elements in the security forces who are arresting protesters, but these actions are condemned by the new prime minister."

Whether he will be able to improve the situation has yet to be seen. Tariq Alturfi, a journalist from Karbala who reports on militia violence and corruption in government, says it is becoming impossible to enforce the law in his city, and pressure is mounting on protesters and secular voices demanding government transparency.

"I may have to leave Iraq soon but, for now, I'm trying to work as much as possible, providing press coverage with my colleagues in Karbala," he said. He is being closely watched but he feels his mission is a duty towards his homeland.

He continued: "They accuse us of working for Saudi Arabia and America, and they say, 'You are inciting against Iran and the local parties'. But we are working impartially, standing with the people, and working on peaceful demonstrations." ⊗

Translated by **Denise Muir**

Laura Silvia Battaglia *is contributing editor to Index for Yemen and Iraq*

MAIN: The death of
a protester at the
hands of the army
sparked riots in
Tripoli, Lebanon in
April 2020

CREDIT: Elizabeth Fitt/Alamy

CULTURE

IN THIS SPECIAL culture section, we present three superb new plays that look at various aspects of what living through a pandemic means, especially when it comes to our freedoms. Written by world-famous writers - V (formerly Eve Ensler), **KATHERINE PARKINSON** and **LUCIEN BOURJEILY** - the plays stand as witness to this pivotal moment in history. All three are published here for the first time.

Masking the truth

Jemimah Steinfeld talks to the writer of The Vagina Monologues about her play in which she imagines a world similar to the Covid-19 restricted one we are living in today

49(02): 76/81 I DOI: 10.1177/0306422020935356

"**WE HAVE ALL** got to guard against surveillance. When they start surveying our bodies in the name of medical diagnosis, imagine what they will be able do next," said the writer V (formerly known as Eve Ensler). V has fought against body policing throughout her career. The Tony award-winning playwright became a household name when she wrote and performed The Vagina Monologues in 1996, with its acerbic look at violence and taboos around female genitalia.

"How is all of this going to get used by fascists and authoritarians, and people who wish to control people and shut down dissent and to influence and divide people and exclude people and eliminate people? It concerns me deeply," she said of the current crisis.

"Once you dislocate people from their bodies – and the body has always been the loci of revolution and change – you take away some fundamental power that they have, and agency and authority over their own life."

We are discussing Chamomile Tea – a new version of a play she first conceived of during the Ronald Reagan years in the USA. The play imagines two women living behind masks as a result of a nuclear fallout. When she originally wrote it – when the president was constantly talking about a winnable nuclear war – V entered a period in which she couldn't eat or sleep, imagining people disappearing "in various ways".

The play is an exploration of one of these scenarios, and while its backdrop is one of nuclear waste, the questions the women ask about freedom could be copied and pasted into today's crisis.

"Will you go out and risk getting ill? Will you live with freedom and potentially die [going outside] or will you live inside a gas mask where you can no longer eat, talk or feel? What is it like living without touch, without connection to people, without community?" she asked.

While she describes Donald Trump's presidency as a "grotesque nightmare", V believes that what we're seeing now is the devastating consequence of the full-throttled neo-liberalism that began with Reagan. It's the result of some people dominating conversations to such an extent that warnings over things such as the environment and, crucially, global pandemics have been ignored.

"So much has become polarised," she said. "In the US, people listen to news media and get absolutely opposing views. Where is truth? What is truth? In my lifetime it has never been so extreme. We're living in a post-truth world, where people don't know what is real and who to trust. We don't have anywhere near a collective understanding of what is true."

She believes that one result is that these "denying powers feed into people's desires to not do anything".

V founded the global protest movement One Billion Rising, which seeks to empower women to speak up against gender-based violence, and at the time of the interview she is deeply troubled by the prospect of not being able to easily protest while restrictions are in place.

"What disturbs me at the moment is that we need to congregate, we need community – movements are based on people coming together in the street, the town hall and meeting places," she said, adding that class and racial divides were diabolically apparent now. Essential workers go to work and risk their lives while the more privileged can take shelter.

RIGHT: Writer and activist V, whose play The Vagina Monologues has been performed in over 140 countries

"Is this going to open the door to the wicked, who are already trying to deregulate everything, already trying to extract every possible inch of this planet and the next, or is this going to bring in a time when care is the most central part of society and we live for people over profits?"

She is deeply concerned about stories that domestic violence has risen during the lockdowns, but it is not just women whose voices are being silenced.

"There's such a judgment of men by other men who really want to talk, to change their bad behaviour and address patriarchy. It is very hard for men to come forward without getting judged or put down," she said, explaining that when she toured the world in 2019 to promote her book, The Apology, many more men were in the audience than she expected and many were interested in a process of reckoning.

Once you dislocate people from their bodies – and the body has always been the loci of revolution and change – you take away some fundamental power

"But there is fear and apprehension," she said. "An apology process is a very good place to begin. Without this I'm not sure we'll end violence towards women." ⊗

Jemimah Steinfeld is deputy editor at Index on Censorship

Chamomile Tea

By V

INT. LIVING ROOM

A woman, Jane, in her 50s/60s is seated on a sofa in a lovely living room. She is surrounded by elegant furniture, an ambience of wealth and sophisticated taste. She is dressed in L.K.Bennett and is wearing a gas mask. The gas mask is decorated with flowers which match her dress. She sits, waiting on the sofa. In a bit, another woman, Eugenie, the same age enters. She is also dressed in L.K.Bennett and is wearing a similar gas mask. She carries a tray of tea sandwiches, a teapot and delicate china cups.

Inside each of their gas masks is a microphone. Initially Eugenie's microphone is turned up too high.

Eugenie speaks as she enters.

EUGENIE   Sorry to make you wait. I never seem to gauge time properly anymore.

JANE   Don't mean to be rude, but your microphone is turned up a bit too high.

Eugenie turns her microphone down by adjusting a switch in her pocket.

→

EUGENIE   I said, sorry to make you wait. I never seem to gauge time properly anymore.

JANE   I know what you mean, dear. Oh look, what a delicious lunch.

EUGENIE   I tried to make you your favourite.

JANE   Well, you have. (She holds up the sandwich in front of her goggle eyes to get a better look at it) Look, tunafish on croissant.

EUGENIE   With onions.

JANE   With onions. It's beautiful.

EUGENIE   And then, your tea.

JANE   It's not chamomile is it?

EUGENIE   Indeed it is.

JANE   What a friend, what a truly good friend you are.

EUGENIE   It was my pleasure. Just to imagine what your face looked like.

JANE   Well, I'll tell you. I'm smiling. I'm excited. There's a tenderness to my eyes and mouth because I am feeling so much love for you.

EUGENIE   Well, I'm pleased back. (Pause) What is it? What thought is that?

JANE   It's not allowed. It's bad.

EUGENIE   Well, say it. Go ahead.

JANE   No, I can't.

EUGENIE   Come on.

JANE   No, no. I can't.

EUGENIE   Oh please!

JANE   Well, what if, what if, imagine if we could eat this food.

EUGENIE   (Angry and hurt) But we agreed. We never would imagine that.

JANE   I know. I said it was bad.

EUGENIE   But we said never. I thought we meant never.

JANE   You asked me what I was thinking.

EUGENIE   You didn't have to tell me.

JANE   Well, you didn't have to make tuna and onion sandwiches on croissant with chamomile tea.

EUGENIE   I thought it would make you happy.

JANE   (Begins to cry) Well, it did make me happy.

EUGENIE   What are you doing?

JANE   I am crying. Inside of here I am crying and it has no place to go.

EUGENIE   Oh no. You must stop crying. You cannot cry. If your nose runs it's a dreadful mess.

JANE   I feel lousy.

EUGENIE   Well, you mustn't. We must think of something cheerful, something to get your mind off this.

Eugenie sniffles.

EUGENIE   (CONT'D) Please, please. You mustn't. (She tickles her arm. Jane giggles) Come on.

JANE   Stop. (She giggles more) Stop. Oh no. I'm steaming up.

Her goggles are all steamed up. Eugenie takes out her purse-sized Windex spray.

EUGENIE   I'll clean you off.

She sprays Jane's goggles and cleans them off.

JANE   Thank you, Eugenie.

They both take out needlepoint and

CREDIT: Kerry Roper/Ikon

begin to sew.

EUGENIE I've had to restart this thing about six times. I just can't concentrate the way I used to. My mind wanders off and before you know it I've been gone for hours, sometimes days.

JANE Oh God, I know what you mean. Yesterday I was cleaning the kitchen floor. Our cleaning friend has not been well. I was mopping away and the next thing I knew I was on the shelf of my bedroom closet, dusting. I don't remember how I got

→ there. What are you making? The yarn is beautiful.

EUGENIE Well, it began as a shawl for Sheri, but you never know what it will become these days. What are you working on?

JANE It's a pillow for the couch. (She holds it up to show her. In needlepoint it reads, "It's Better Here Than There.")

EUGENIE (Reading it) It's better here than there. Lovely. What does it mean?

JANE Goodness, I don't know. I really don't know.

EUGENIE (Quick. Catching herself) No matter. Don't know why I asked.

JANE It's a reasonable question, I hadn't thought...

EUGENIE It was a slip. That's all. A slip.

JANE What do you mean?

EUGENIE It's not for me to question why, not for me to understand.

JANE Eugenie, what is it?

EUGENIE Would you like more tea?

She fills her cup.

JANE Understand what?

EUGENIE (Totally objective and detached) My granddaughter's been quite sick.

JANE No.

EUGENIE Can you imagine? I tried to understand.

JANE Bone marrow. Is it bone marrow?

EUGENIE (Annoyed) I said she's been quite sick.

JANE I only asked.

EUGENIE Well, don't. It's not your

granddaughter.

JANE No, it's not. Both of mine are gone already.

EUGENIE That was unkind of me.

Jane says nothing, Then she accidentally knocks over the teacup and it breaks.

JANE Oh goodness, I've broken your lovely cup.

EUGENIE It's alright.

JANE (Very upset) Why it's broken straight in half. Everything's breaking straight in half. (She begins to cry)

EUGENIE I'm so sorry, Jane. Please, you cannot cry.

JANE I think we're fools.

EUGENIE Please, you mustn't cry.

JANE We're complete and utter fools.

EUGENIE Jane, it's only a cup. Here, look. I found some roses. They're lovely roses. (She rubs them on her skin)

JANE They're fake.

EUGENIE They're roses.

JANE No, they're fake. They're plastic roses. They're dead. You see? (MORE)

JANE (CONT'D) They're dead. They have never been alive.

EUGENIE Jane, you must hold out. They said it would be hard.

JANE They said it would be a few days. It's been months and months.

EUGENIE (She turns on music) Some Bach? No. Vivaldi. The Four Seasons. It will remind us.

Jane turns the music off.

JANE   I want to talk to you.

EUGENIE   I am listening.

The feeding bell goes off.

EUGENIE   (CONT'D) It's that time. (She takes out a bag filled with needles/injections. She rolls up her sleeve, dabs some alcohol on her arm) Feed me, please. (Jane pops the needle in) Thanks. Now, you. (Jane doesn't move) Roll up your sleeve.

JANE   I want to speak to you.

EUGENIE   You must be hungry, dear.

JANE   Face to face.

EUGENIE   What are you saying?

JANE   I want to speak to you.

EUGENIE   You're just hungry.

JANE   I want to rub my eyes.

EUGENIE   You can't. That's all. You can't.

JANE   I want to wash my face. I want to blow my nose.

EUGENIE   Let's play gin rummy. You love gin rummy. (She takes out cards)

JANE   I want to speak to you.

EUGENIE   (Angry, snapping) Now, that's enough.

JANE   You've always been afraid.

EUGENIE   I'm willing to wait.

JANE   To die in masks. To die in someone else's head.

EUGENIE   They say we are spared the worst of it.

JANE   The babies are gone.

EUGENIE   Their cells multiply faster. We are older.

JANE   You always obeyed. When we were younger, you always obeyed.

EUGENIE   Rules protect us.

JANE   You've always been afraid. We are dying and even now the rules make us believe we are not dying.

EUGENIE   I need a nap.

JANE   I am starving.

EUGENIE   Roll up your sleeve.

JANE   I am starving. (She begins to undo her mask)

EUGENIE   What are you doing?

JANE   I need to speak to you and I am starving.

EUGENIE   You are being really silly now.

Jane continues to undo her mask.

EUGENIE   (CONT'D) Stop it, Jane! Stop it!

Jane takes off her mask.

JANE   Oh God. My face. It's mine. (She grabs Eugenie's hand and makes her feel her face) Do you remember me?

EUGENIE   I will be alone now.

JANE   Feel my cheeks, they're flushed.

EUGENIE   You are leaving and I will be alone now.

JANE   Oh, Eugenie. (She ravenously eats the croissant) There were onions after all.

Black out. End of play.

....

V *is a Tony Awards-winning playwright, performer and activist. She is the author of The Vagina Monologues*

Time out

Actor and writer **Katherine Parkinson** talks to **Rachael Jolley** about digital challenges, time off and her new play

49(02):82/90 | DOI: 10.1177/0306422020935358

"**WE ARE HAVING** to connect a lot more on things like FaceTime and so on, so it lends itself quite readily to a playlet," said actor and writer Katherine Parkinson of her new work.

About Face was written specially for this issue of Index, and comes after the successful launch of her playwriting career with Sitting, which went to the Edinburgh Festival Fringe last year.

Parkinson, most famous for her acting in TV hits including The IT Crowd and Humans, is addicted to the theatre. She was in the middle of a run at London's Royal Court when the lockdown happened and stages were closed.

Her new play uses humour to examine how we can reinvent ourselves online – a theme that was born out of her fascination with online dating.

She said that her dating life was pre-internet, so the idea of how it worked online now was one she wanted to explore.

"I'm old enough never to have done any of that and met my husband quite young and met him in the flesh, and I think it is really intriguing that it is becoming quite commonplace for people to meet online," she said.

"In a way you have more choice; you can be more specific in your hunt for the right match.

"I am intrigued by what that does in terms of you meeting somebody online [and] not being able to smell them and see them up close."

The characters in About Face are getting ready for a digital date and the audience observes them making decisions about how they want to present themselves to possible partners.

Parkinson has been getting to grips with new technology a lot more (time for an IT Crowd joke there), and so having her characters meet

using it was a natural step. "I have been doing quite a lot of FaceTime with my mum, so I sat down and wrote it."

The mum is a central character in About Face so it is perhaps not surprising that Parkinson's own mother was part of the inspiration for the writing.

But About Face is mostly about image, what we think about ourselves and how we want others to see us and whether we choose different filters to show ourselves in a different light.

Parkinson seems to have a love-hate relationship with social media and digital tools. She has kept off Twitter because "I know I would be too tempted to do a kind of completely phoney version of myself".

But, as we discuss, there were plenty of ways to change your image even before online dating, such as adding a new haircut or even using a different name for your date.

"That's slightly explored in the piece, because who is the same with their mother as they are with their lover? I think I've always felt I have very different versions whoever I am with," she said.

"I'm a different person when I am with friends. You exist according to your perception with the other person a bit.

"My reality growing up was meeting people in pubs and bars, and I can remember being quite quick to chat to a guy who said he was a pilot and he wasn't a pilot."

So are we using the same tools and techniques online as have been called into play for hundreds of years? "It's quite easy to judge meeting people online as strange, but actually really how different is it from what we have always done? Once you get to know somebody then you are able to be your full self."

One major difference is how the internet platforms where we meet new people have their own tactics and techniques, such as data-scraping – something that pubs were much less adept at doing. But, as Parkinson points out, the information they gather has a truth to it:

ABOVE: The actor and writer Katherine Parkinson

Who is the same with their mother as they are with their lover? I think I've always felt I have very different versions whoever I am with

they know the holidays you are actually booking rather than the ones you tell people you are going on.

"You can chat to someone online and put out whatever image you want, but when you google 'holidays in Cornwall' or 'huskies' then that's your true interests expressing yourself."

So how is she coping with the lockdown and is she reading a lot? "I think any kind of culture is important right now, as it helps to process what is happening and get things in perspective. We've been watching a bit of Blue Planet. I think if I just listen to the bulletins and the numbers and the statistics and so on, I quickly get down about it all."

And there's a lot of reading to be done.

"Reading has never been more significant in my life to stay sane," she said.

She is optimistic that plays will be back, though it's not clear when that will be allowed. "I don't think theatre is ever going to be away for long, and unfortunately I am quite in love with doing it, so I hope it will be back."

But, for now, she is looking forward to performing in an upcoming radio play of Shoe Lady for the BBC, and trying her hand at growing some peas in her garden. ⊗

Rachael Jolley is editor-in-chief of Index on Censorship

About Face

By Katherine Parkinson

INT. BEDROOM/KITCHEN/ STUDY

Sarah, Janet and Damien are all self-isolating in their respective homes. When they FaceTime they speak out to the audience, as if it is the computer screen.

SARAH	It doesn't matter what trousers I wear, Mum, he'll only see me from the waist up.
JANET	But leggings! It looks like you've given up.
SARAH	Given up what? Jeans?
JANET	Life, Sarah. Life, love. Sex.
SARAH	I was ringing for reassurance.
JANET	You look gorgeous, darling. In your usual low-key way.
SARAH	Right.
JANET	Have you put something on your lips?
SARAH	Just some lip gloss.
JANET	Yes, they look different.

SARAH	Tinted lip gloss.
JANET	They look a bit sore.
SARAH	Oh no, do they?
JANET	Just a bit. Are they sore?
SARAH	No, Mum, it's lip tint.
JANET	They look a bit blue. Maybe it's my screen. You haven't been picking at them? You know we aren't supposed to be touching our faces at all if we can help it.
SARAH	I'll take it off.

She wipes the back of her hand over her lips to get it off.

JANET	Don't touch your face!
SARAH	Sorry. I'll wash my hands.

Sarah exits. Janet continues to stare at the empty screen. Then shouts.

JANET	SARAH?

Sarah returns to Janet's vision, drying her hands on her leggings.

SARAH	I'm here, Mum. I was washing my hands.
JANET	I didn't know where you'd gone.
SARAH	I was in the bathroom.
JANET	I thought you'd been taken.
SARAH	You always think the worst.
JANET	Because the worst has happened.
SARAH	I know you don't like it when I just use the gel.
JANET	Don't dry them on your leggings, you'll give your legs the virus too.
SARAH	I don't think it works like that.
JANET	Oh, your lips look much more normal now.
SARAH	Good. I'm panicking because he's never

→	seen me before.
JANET	He's seen your photo, hasn't he? You said you'd seen his.
SARAH	Yes, but he hasn't seen me in real life.
JANET	Is FaceTime real life?
SARAH	The photo was very edited.
JANET	You do suit black and white.
SARAH	I used filters.
JANET	You suit them.
SARAH	Will he think I'm not as nice as the picture?
JANET	Nobody is as nice as their picture, darling.
SARAH	You're making me feel worse.
JANET	He might be grotesque.
SARAH	I might cancel.
JANET	It's only a video call.
SARAH	I'm not ready to date, anyway.
JANET	Maybe you shouldn't be on dating sites, then.
SARAH	You told me to be on them.
JANET	You don't even use your real name.
SARAH	Everyone lies online, Mum. It's expected.
JANET	It's false advertising.
SARAH	It's advertising.
JANET	Be yourself.
SARAH	Why?
JANET	Because no version of you could be better than you.
SARAH	Mum. What a lovely thing to say.
JANET	But maybe wear a mask.
SARAH	What?
JANET	In case he's a psychopath.
SARAH	My Donald Trump mask?
JANET	No. Although that one IS very funny.
SARAH	My corona mask?
JANET	Pretend you've just got back from the shops. And haven't had time to take it off.
SARAH	What's wrong with him seeing my face?
JANET	A mask will keep you mysterious, to protect you. He's a stranger. Off the internet.
SARAH	He'd only see half of my face.
JANET	Which half?
SARAH	The top half. Obviously.
JANET	Isn't that the half you're worried about?
SARAH	No, Mum. I quite like that half.
JANET	He might be wearing a mask, too.
SARAH	I doubt it.
JANET	In the current climate.
SARAH	Indoors?
JANET	Did he have one in his photo?
SARAH	No.
JANET	You said he had a beard.
SARAH	A beard, and no mask.
JANET	Why are people still not wearing masks?
SARAH	It's a dating website, Mum.
JANET	If you can't get one, improvise.
SARAH	He did say he was struggling to get one on Amazon.
JANET	I've seen people in Waitrose with knickers on their face.
SARAH	Could've been him.
JANET	What else do you know about him?
SARAH	He's my age.
JANET	Oh.
SARAH	He's a lab technician.
JANET	Oh.
SARAH	He has a dog.

JANET What sort?

SARAH Husky.

JANET You like huskies, don't you?

SARAH I do. I mean that's kind of why I clicked on him. He was holding it in the photo.

JANET And you had a chat?

SARAH We had a great online chat, yes. About whether dogs carry the virus.

JANET Lovely. Do they?

SARAH I can't remember.

JANET What colour was it?

SARAH Brown, with flecks.

JANET The beard?

SARAH The husky.

JANET Oh. Beard?

SARAH Ginger.

JANET Ah.

SARAH Do you think my mouth looks weird? I'm worried he'll think I have a weird mouth.

JANET What are you talking about? You have a lovely mouth. Is it your teeth you're worried about?

Sarah notices Damien is FaceTiming her.

SARAH What? My teeth? No, I wasn't worried about my teeth, what's wrong with my-

Sarah ends her FaceTime call with Janet. Janet wipes down her computer screen with cleaning product and proceeds to wipe down other surfaces through the following, waiting for her daughter to call back.

We hear the ring of the new incoming

FaceTime call. Sarah goes to reapply the lip gloss but then doesn't. She checks her teeth in her image on the screen. She messes her hair to look casual but then tidies it again and frantically answers the call.

She tries to talk without revealing her teeth.

SARAH (CONT'D) Oh, hi!

Damien calls from a small box room.

DAMIEN Hey Elvira.

SARAH I completely forgot about our scheduled call!

DAMIEN You forgot? No problem. Is this a busy time for you because I know you said you had a video conference call today?

SARAH No, it's cool. I've just ended the meeting.

DAMIEN I can call you back?

SARAH I have a window. In my schedule. Nice to meet you, Damien.

DAMIEN Nice to meet you too, Elvira. In the flesh.

SARAH The digital flesh.

DAMIEN You look exactly like your photo. But in colour. And moving.

SARAH Do I? Good. I hate the way some people use filters and so on. It's just false advertising.

DAMIEN I know what you mean, Elvira.

SARAH Mmm. How is the lockdown treating you, Damien?

DAMIEN I'm struggling to get motivated today, if I'm honest. I haven't even done Joe Wicks.

SARAH He does get a bit samey.

DAMIEN Especially if you watch the same one every day!

SARAH Yes, I just watch, too. I don't think many people actually DO it.

DAMIEN Right. Ha.

Sarah smiles and then remembers to hide her teeth, and so ends up doing a strange grimace.

DAMIEN (CONT'D) Sarah, are you OK? You seem to be in pain.

SARAH No, I'm not in pain. But thanks for asking. I mean obviously we are all in pain in the present circumstances.

DAMIEN Strange times.

JANET Strange times.

Janet is FaceTiming Sarah again.

SARAH I'm so sorry. I have another call.

DAMIEN No problem. Go ahead and take it.

SARAH Do you mind staying there?

DAMIEN No.

SARAH I'll only be a minute.

DAMIEN I won't go anywhere.

SARAH They're calling from New York, you see.

DAMIEN I shall stay put.

Sarah takes the incoming call.

JANET Well?

SARAH Mum.

JANET How was it?

SARAH Why are you calling?

JANET How was the date?

SARAH I'm still talking to him.

JANET No, it's me darling. You're talking to me.

SARAH I know.

JANET Can't you see me?

SARAH I can see you.

JANET I can see you, too. Your hair looks a bit messy, maybe smooth it down.

Sarah smooths her hair down with her hand.

JANET (CONT'D) Not with your hand!

Sarah grabs a pillow with her teeth and uses it like a brush.

SARAH Let me get back to him.

JANET Is he very ginger?

SARAH Does my hair look better now?

JANET It really does, darling.

SARAH Thanks.

JANET Remind him to get a mask.

Sarah reconnects with Damien.

DAMIEN Hey.

SARAH Hey.

DAMIEN I haven't gone anywhere, like I promised.

SARAH Staying home saves lives.

DAMIEN That too.
Your hair's changed.

SARAH Has it? Yes. It was a work colleague in Berlin, so I had to be presentable.

DAMIEN I thought you said New York?

SARAH He's from Berlin, he's in New York.

DAMIEN	I hope I'm not interrupting calls from colleagues.
SARAH	No, not a colleague, more a friend. A colleague-cum-friend. Not a cum-friend! I mean a friendly colleague.
DAMIEN	Right. Yes, I have those, too. Friendly colleagues, I mean.

Sarah is embarrassed.

DAMIEN (CONT'D)	Do you do all your video conference calls in your bedroom?
SARAH	Yes. It's good to stay connected during this time.
DAMIEN	You've got a really nice bedroom.
SARAH	Thanks.
DAMIEN	I love the green wallpaper.
SARAH	It's blue.
DAMIEN	I should probably connect with people a bit more.
SARAH	We all need to connect.
DAMIEN	I'm a natural self-isolator, I think.
SARAH	Well, we're connecting now, aren't we?

A beat.

DAMIEN	Yes. I think we are.
SARAH	Your beard.
DAMIEN	Yes.
SARAH	You've lost it.
DAMIEN	Literally no idea where I've put it.
SARAH	I couldn't work out what it was that was different from your photo.
DAMIEN	Wearing a mask over a beard is itchy.
SARAH	You managed to get one?
DAMIEN	I made one, like you suggested.

From a pillowcase.

He produces his homemade mask and puts it on.

SARAH	Ha.

He keeps it on.

SARAH (CONT'D)	How's your dog?
DAMIEN	About her. I don't know how to tell you this.
SARAH	Oh, I'm so sorry!
DAMIEN	She's not dead.
SARAH	Thank God.
DAMIEN	No, she's not hurt, she's just not mine.
SARAH	What?
DAMIEN	She belongs to a friend.
SARAH	Oh.
DAMIEN	I walk her occasionally.
SARAH	Your friend?
DAMIEN	The dog. Right.
SARAH (CONT'D)	Do you have a dog?
DAMIEN	No.
SARAH	Have you ever had a dog, Damien?
DAMIEN	No.
SARAH	Are you called Damien?

Damien pulls down his mask.

DAMIEN	Yes.
SARAH	Why did you lie?
DAMIEN	I don't know, Elvira.
SARAH	Well, you suit a dog.
DAMIEN	Thanks.
SARAH	I should go.
DAMIEN	Yes, I'm sure you're really busy. →

SARAH — I am. I'm finding it a weirdly productive time, actually.

DAMIEN — Me too. Totally. But also quite boring.

SARAH — Quite boring.

They laugh.

DAMIEN — Maybe we could meet up and social distance some time?

SARAH — I'd like that, Damien.

They end the call.
The three sit in silence.
Sarah calls Janet.

JANET — Well?

SARAH — Well, I liked him.

JANET — Wonderful!

SARAH — I mean, he lied about having a dog.

JANET — Oh. But he seemed normal?

SARAH — Yes, normal.

JANET — Although even the psychopaths seem normal.

SARAH — He didn't seem like a psychopath.

JANET — It's so hard to tell when it's just a screen.

SARAH — I liked him, Mum.

JANET — It must be strange nowadays doing everything remotely, even sexual things.

SARAH — I didn't have sex with him, Mum.

JANET — How are people continuing affairs? I feel for them really.

SARAH — I felt a strong connection.

JANET — The wifi is very good where you are.

SARAH — He was nice.

JANET — It's impossible to feel any chemistry, I suppose.

SARAH — But we chat for hours like this, Mum.

JANET — Yes, but I'm talking about the electricity between lovers, the *je ne sais quoi*. We had it in droves, me and your father. DROVES.

SARAH — I know you did, Mum.

JANET — I miss him, Sarah.

SARAH — I know.

Janet is crying.

JANET — I hate that it happened without me there, without me holding his hand.

SARAH — The nurse held his hand, Mum.

JANET — It should have been me.

SARAH — He knew you couldn't be there.

JANET — Do you think he knew?

SARAH — He knew we loved him, Mum.

Sarah reaches out to touch the screen.

SARAH (CONT'D) — That's what love does.

Janet reaches out, too.

JANET — I love you, Sarah.

SARAH — I know you do, Mum.

....

Katherine Parkinson *is a playwright and actor*

Life in action

Lebanese playwright **Lucien Bourjeily** talks to **Orna Herr** about a new play he has written exclusively for Index

49(02): 91/97 I DOI: 10.1177/0306422020935359

"**IT'S ABOUT HOW** much you are willing to sacrifice," said Lucien Bourjeily, the Lebanese stage director, filmmaker and author of The Video, a playlet written exclusively for this magazine.

"Is it hopeful? I would say it's realistic," he told Index.

"If you are a pessimist, I would say you'll see it in a pessimistic way. If you are an optimist, you will see it in an optimistic way – that there is hope."

Despite spanning just minutes of two characters' lives, The Video captures the nuances of their world views. Salim, an activist who posted – then quickly deleted – a video of himself decrying the death of a protester at the hands of the army, is anxious after discovering it has gone viral. His friend, Walid, sees the positive difference Salim's words could make.

The Video encapsulates an atmosphere of censorship, the fear of repercussions for speaking out, dismay at how the coronavirus lockdown is being used by the authorities to crush dissent, and belief that activism can make a difference. It is a Pandora's box – hope is present among apparent abject hopelessness.

Does the playlet hold up a mirror to the current situation in Lebanon, where there have been protests since October 2019 and which, at the time of writing, is on Covid lockdown?

"It was very noticeable that they used the health emergency, which is of course a very serious one, but I mean they used it to enforce things that they couldn't do before ... imprisoning people and even torturing people. They used torture against protesters which is something you didn't hear about in the last

five months before Covid-19, so they increased the level of brutality," Bourjeily said.

Through The Video, Bourjeily also examines censorship through what he calls "psychological violence".

Salim deleted his video after receiving confrontational comments online, and Bourjeily knows from experience the impact these can have.

"Because I believe in freedom of expression I've never blocked anybody in my life, but you wouldn't imagine the comments I get on Twitter," he said. "Some people cannot take it, and this is what the government and people in power know is effective. People think that oppression is only about a policeman with a baton hitting you on the head. It's not only that."

However, Bourjeily's work is starkly honest about the dangers activists face. Salim's anxiety about his anti-establishment video going viral is not played as cowardice but as pragmatism. Bourjeily says the playlet speaks to the inner conflict every activist and protester has: "How hard will I be willing to go or to sacrifice for my ideas?"

They feel that change is so difficult, so costly, it might affect their daily lives or they might be killed. So, are they willing to take that chance?

"There hasn't been any kind of big change in any country in the world unless some people in one way or another sacrificed the most precious thing, which was their lives," he said. "This is the ultimate censorship – they are killed. The ultimate censorship is when somebody actually dies because they are trying to advocate →

People think that oppression is only about a policeman with a baton hitting you on the head. It's not only that

ABOVE: Award-winning playwright Lucien Bourjeily

→ certain ideas or certain changes or certain political aspirations."

But Bourjeily, who is currently working on Vanishing, a film about a journalist investigating the disappearance of her friend, ended on a positive note on the future.

"There is hope because, ultimately, history tells us that such oppression cannot last forever," he said. ⊗

Orna Herr *is editorial assistant at Index on Censorship*

The Video

By Lucien Bourjeily

Salim, 45, sits on a small toilet seat browsing through his phone. The bathroom is of compact size, barely fitting his large, tall body.

Suddenly, he gets a WhatsApp notification.

He clicks on it and a video plays.

VOICE FROM VIDEO Greetings to you all my compatriots, I am making this video to...

Salim zaps through the video.

VOICE FROM VIDEO The army isn't supposed to be facing off the people protesting... it's not the army who are a red line it's the people who are hungry... the killing of this young father who was protesting for the basic right of citizens in this country is but a reminder that the government is a criminal one and should be fought with all means possible... there is a small child who is now fatherless because...

He holds the phone and pushes on it with his thumb and speaks into the mic.

SALIM Morning Walid. How did the video reach you?

A beep confirming the message was sent, then Salim takes a long and deep breath. He then calls a number and puts the phone on speaker mode.

WALID Morning!

SALIM Sorry to call you at this hour.

WALID All is well?

SALIM Fine, fine... not really fine to be honest. I just left you a message...

WALID Absolutely... how can anyone be fine stuck at home like this? I think we might die first of stress and anxiety before corona!

There are many noises coming in from the phone and the connection is bad.

WALID   Salim, I can barely hear you. There are a lot of echoes.

Loud children's noises can be heard from Walid's house through the phone. Salim stands up, puts his clothes back on, and steps out of the bathroom and into the living room.

He holds the phone closer to his mouth and paces up and down the room while talking.

SALIM   (*Louder*) Better?

WALID   Yes, much better. The kids are making so much noise here. Wait a second, let me go to the balcony.

The sounds of kids fade off.

WALID   Wouldn't have imagined the day when the balcony would become less noisy than inside the house.

Silence.

WALID   Yes, tell me …

SALIM   The video: how did you get it?

WALID   The family WhatsApp group I guess, oh no, wait… I actually got it from a pro-revolution broadcast group. It's being shared a lot. No?

SALIM   I…

WALID   I couldn't believe that was you! Such a powerful video my friend, it really made my blood boil. These corrupt motherfuckers are really sucking us dry: they don't allow people to make a living, nor to protest, nor do they give out proper financial support.

SALIM   So, you know who sent it?

WALID   Not really. There are almost 200 people in that group and they forward a million things each day.

SALIM   Ah, OK.

WALID   What's bothering you?

SALIM   It's that… I deleted this video on Facebook two days ago.
I published it, then I deleted it like half an hour later. Suddenly, today, I get it back from you here.
Someone must have downloaded and started sending it on WhatsApp.

WALID   But why did you delete it? It's an excellent video, really!
You summarised it all perfectly: how they are using the corona lockdown to consolidate their power, the story of the protester who died by a rubber bullet, and all said in a very spontaneous and emotional way.

SALIM   I haven't got the 400,000 *liras* that they promised to give out to all people affected by the lockdown.
It's been more than two weeks and everyone in this street got them except me, and the barber at the corner of the street.
Why? Is it because he and I are both vocal and critical of the establishment?

WALID This money, for food and basic support, is supposed to be for everyone and not taking into consideration party allegiance.

(Sarcastic)

This is what they said on TV.

SALIM Yeah right.

WALID So, you criticised the very people who are supposed to be giving you the "coupon"?

SALIM Yes, and I feel this is the reason why they are not giving me the 400,000 *liras* which I am perfectly entitled to.

Beat.

WALID This could be a scandal if well evidenced.

SALIM If... but how can you prove it?

WALID Impossible or almost... But still... it's such a shame you deleted the video. Every Lebanese should see it.

SALIM And then what?

WALID And then... and then they get incited to do something instead of just sitting home, playing with their toes, getting poorer by the day, while their money in the banks is getting literally stolen, and all their savings illegally confiscated.

SALIM But do what? Protest during the lockdown? Some people did it and we saw how it ended.

WALID It ended badly because they used excessive force against them. And,

RIGHT: A protester walks the deserted streets of Beirut, Lebanon

of course, because not enough people are protesting and we are all afraid of large groupings.

SALIM Yes, but more importantly nobody cared! Did you check the media? They barely covered the story. That was one more reason that got me

CREDIT: Joseph Eid/Getty

infuriated!

The guy died while protesting the living conditions, corruption, and devaluating *lira* while all TV stations were broadcasting a romantic series!

WALID   Mimi, don't open the door!

You are not wearing any shoes, stay inside!

SALIM   They used it very cleverly in a progressive manner: first, they removed all the protesters' tents – which were mostly empty anyway – then they started taking people from their →

→ homes to be detained, then they brutally repressed protests. And the news stayed only about corona.

In the current lockdown if they execute people in the middle of the street, no one would rise up against it.

People would barely come to the funeral!

WALID But there's social media…

SALIM OK, they share it on social media, watch it, and get angry for a moment but then what?

They forget it after a couple of minutes or a maximum of an hour and move on.

Finally, it's me in the video not them! My life will be forever affected and not their lives.

WALID I'm really surprised to hear you say that! This is a 180 degree U-turn from what you said in the video.

One viral video released and you've suddenly become a typical Lebanese politician!

SALIM The quarantine effect…

WALID You made it sound like those who shared the video on WhatsApp are condemning you to a life sentence of misery.

Let's put it in perspective: in the past, there have been many other people who shared somehow similar political videos and they are still alive… and kicking.

SALIM I really need this money! For 10 days now they have been telling me each time: call us back tomorrow.

I called the municipality, three mayors, the army, even the offices of political parties but none got back to me. My name is not on "the list". How to add it to "the list"? No one knows.

When I put the video on Facebook, five minutes later I started getting comments and messages from government and army supporters about the "sanctity of the army", "the army is a red line", the army this, the army that… I think the most unnerving one was "your army is right even if it oppresses you".

WALID What the fuck have these guys been smoking? "We oppress you for your own protection." They hit you, detain you, and even kill you and in the end they make you feel that you should be grateful for their "kindness".

SALIM A young man was needlessly dead, and these people were aggressively defending the army and those in power, it's so absurd!

Let's at least applaud them for something: the government is very proficient in switching things around and making the people feel as if they are the cruel oppressors and that those in power are the soft-hearted oppressed.

WALID What a mindfuck.

SALIM I couldn't sleep before deleting it. I swear I started sweating like crazy as if I ran a whole marathon. I suddenly couldn't get the 400,000 *liras* out of my head, and that I might have lost them for good.

Look, if I was sure my video will make a difference I would have left it and sacrificed for it. But unfortunately, I felt I just hurt myself and didn't help anyone, this is what raced in my mind as soon as I posted it.

WALID It's a gamble, of course, and if I put myself in your shoes I am not sure what I would have done. But think about what are you risking? Other people already lost their lives, or limbs, or loved ones.

I agree this video might not make one iota of difference in the greater scheme of things but its true impact simply can't be measured.

In an ongoing uprising, we cannot predict which speech, which video, or which death will be the straw that breaks the camel's back.

I still remember the Egyptian revolution there was a video of a middle-aged man in the street, very emotionally charged, I can still remember his face even after years of watching it.

He was just saying that he could not take it anymore that they had suffered more than they can endure, he cried and ripped part of his shirt off. A very simple video but it travelled the world and I watched it and I remember very well when I did that I felt that Mubarak will fall.

I felt it: this video will galvanise

millions in Egypt and it somehow did. It didn't do it by itself but it was a part of the final push. A straightforward but heartfelt video.

Silence.

WALID Salim, still there? I feel I've talked too much as usual. Yara, Mimi, both of you: stop stomping on the floor, it's too early, the neighbours will come and knock on our door again!

SALIM No, my bad. I'm sorry I bothered with all this so early in the morning. Look at me I'm all sweaty again, this stress is killing me.

Salim's phone vibrates.

SALIM Just a second, I'm getting a call.

WALID Call me later if you want.

SALIM It's a "Private Number"...

WALID Fuck!

Lights out.

....

Lucien Bourjeily *is a Lebanese writer and director of both theatre and film. His work has been featured at worldwide festival circuits and won him many awards, including the 2017 Dubai International Film Festival Jury Prize*

INDEX AROUND THE WORLD

Putting abuse on the map

Orna Herr reports on Index's first digital awards ceremony and the launch of a new mapping project

49(02): 98/100 | DOI: 10.1177/0306422020935365

"**PRESS FREEDOM IS** critical at any time – and in particular during a pandemic. Knowledge is not just power, it is a matter of life or death for someone," said Jemimah Steinfeld, deputy editor of Index on Censorship magazine, commenting on the mapping project that Index has launched. "We need to rally behind those whose job it is to inform us."

In many countries around the world, the coronavirus pandemic has been used to try to restrict the right to report.

Between 18 March and the time of writing, more than 150 incidents had already been logged by the mapping and monitoring project, which was set up by Mark Frary, associate editor at Index.

"When it comes to times of crisis, those attacks increase," he said, citing the examples of General Abdel Fattah el-Sisi seizing power in Egypt in 2013 and the failed coup in Turkey in 2016.

"What happens is that those governments, whoever succeeded in that crisis… often use that as an excuse to clamp down on the media who have previously held them to account.

"When opposition voices, and journalists who report on those opposition voices, are not able to shine the light on those in power, then the hard-won freedom that we have in society can very quickly be eroded."

And Frary believes patterns have emerged in these recent attacks on media freedom.

"I think that one of the things that has come through is how governments are saying that only state-approved media can report on coronavirus. That's happened in a few places," he said. "For example, there was a case in Liberia recently where the government said, 'We're rescinding all of the press cards that have been issued by the press union of Liberia', and they've only reissued them to state-owned media. That's not an isolated incident."

Journalists and activists, now more than ever, are faced with governments that want to censor vital information. To highlight some of those cases, Index embraced innovation with determination to host the 20th annual Freedom of Expression Awards, despite the pandemic. The event was originally set to be held in April at the May Fair hotel in London.

Writer, presenter and Index contributor Timandra Harkness hosted the awards from her home, with a live blog, tweets and Instagram posts revealing the winners and their acceptance speech videos throughout the day on 16 April.

Harkness said there were silver linings to be found in the cloud of being unable to hold a physical ceremony.

"Rather than concentrating all the love and appreciation into one evening with food and drink, maybe we can continue it in our everyday lives a bit longer," she said. "Flatten the curve of appreciation.

"The whole point of the awards, whether it's live from my living room or in a much more festive setting, is to remind everybody how important it is to do this work, and that people have, in some cases, taken personal risks and certainly worked very hard to defend freedom of expression."

Leah Cross, Index's senior events and partnership manager, said: "One huge benefit was that moving the announcement online made the awards more accessible, and enabled us to have a much bigger reach than a live event. As the awards celebrate those fighting censorship around the world, it was wonderful to dedicate a whole day to the nominees and winners,

sharing their stories through video."

There were five winners over the four categories, with joint winners in the campaigning category.

Sayed Ahmed Alwadaei, a Bahraini activist now living in exile in the UK, was one of the campaigning winners for his work with the Bahrain Institute for Rights and Democracy. Harkness said she found Alwadaei particularly inspiring as he "used his recorded acceptance speech to remind us all about his friend Nabeel [Rajab], himself a former Index awardee, who is currently in prison in Bahrain for criticising the government on Twitter. A reminder that we need both personal courage and solidarity with others to win this fight for free speech".

In an interview with Index, Alwadaei described how much winning the award meant to him and fellow Bahrainis.

"This is something I feel very proud of," he said. "Firstly it is a recognition of the important work the organisation does, but also it is something that would make my own country very proud. I get a lot of messages from people expressing their happiness about it."

He also talked about the difference the award would make to his work.

"As a local NGO, sometimes it's really hard to express yourself strongly – but if you are being recognised and receiving an international award, that says quite a lot," he said. "It's something that helps the recognition of our work and [helps us to] reach out in a much more effective way."

He said that the coronavirus pandemic at first proved to be a challenge to the work Bird

Journalists and activists, now more than ever, are faced with governments that want to censor vital information

did, but then it became an opportunity to draw attention to issues that might have otherwise been ignored.

For example, the group pitched a story to Reuters explaining that an outbreak of coronavirus in Bahraini prisons would be "some sort of life sentence" for the prisoners, many of whom are human rights activists.

Alwadaei continued: "We were also able to mobilise with international organisations to shed light about the challenges those prisoners face."

Attacks on freedom of expression are not restricted to authoritarian countries. There are several reports on the Index map of US President Donald Trump verbally attacking journalists, either during press briefings or on Twitter.

Hana Meihan Davis, a member of Index's youth advisory board currently living in →

ABOVE: Downloading a Covid tracking app is mandatory for government employees in India

That's very alarming for most of the countries in the COE which are democratic, or purport to be democracies

ABOVE: US President Donald Trump speaks at a campaign rally in Arizona, USA. The president is known for showing open contempt towards members of the media

→ the USA, said: "Trump's attack on liberal media, his delayed response to the Covid-19 outbreak... have only fuelled the devastation caused by the virus.

"Now, driven by Trump-approved accounts of the situation, the president's supporters fight for the full reopening of the country, while others are left to wonder when the sickness and fear will end."

As well as attacks on media freedom, Index is covering attacks on privacy through the increased surveillance conducted in the name of coronavirus. In India, downloading the tracking app Aarogya Setu is mandatory for government employees.

Youth advisory board member Satyabhama Rajoria, from Madhya Pradesh, said: "While the app can help to trace the cases of Covid-19, it can also potentially act as a surveillance system which can be misused. It is a potential threat to our right to privacy."

This theme is explored in depth in the special report in this magazine.

While there has been a spike in attacks on media freedom during the pandemic, it is just part of a trend throughout the world in recent years.

Index was one of the partner organisations to the recently published annual report on the Council of Europe Platform to Promote the Protection of Journalism and the Protection of Journalists. The report analyses alerts filed on the Council of Europe's platform.

Index's senior policy research and advocacy officer, Jessica Ní Mhainín, said: "I think it's always important to look back and take account of violations that happened over the past 12 months and also to compare them with previous reports... to understand what trends are in place."

A particularly concerning section of the report is on the number of alerts relating to impunity for those who murder journalists.

Ní Mhainín said: "There are 22 cases of impunity, meaning that there was essentially not full justice given to the journalists who were killed... I think that's very alarming for most of the countries in the COE which are democratic, or purport to be democracies."

Ní Mhainín also observed that the report "acknowledged the significant rise in legal threats and judicial and administrative harassment against journalists in Europe".

This ties in with a recently published Index report Ní Mhainín worked on covering how law suits are used against investigate journalists in the EU, the UK and Norway.

Ní Mhainín said the report provided a review of the legal systems in the 29 countries "that are being abused in favour of the powerful", resulting in journalists being subjected to vexatious lawsuits brought by private individuals or companies intended to silence them.

Media freedom is being attacked globally in myriad ways and the situation is worsening in the wake of the coronavirus pandemic.

"It's easy to lose sight in an emergency of other important issues," said Harkness. "But the struggle for freedom of expression doesn't go away just because we have a pandemic – in many ways it's more important than ever." ⊗

Orna Herr is the Tim Hetherington fellow at Index on Censorship

END NOTE

Forced out of the closet

Jemimah Steinfeld talks to LGBTQ people around the world about privacy in dating apps, how the pandemic has accentuated risks and how lives are at stake

49(02): 101/104 I DOI: 10.1177/0306422020935360

FOR MILLIONS OF people, LGBTQ dating apps are the only way to meet new people on a romantic, sexual or social level right now, so a rise in homophobia online is particularly problematic.

Even before the coronavirus pandemic, the popularity of these apps was growing. A Pew Research Centre study this year showed that around half of lesbian, gay and bisexual people in the USA had used dating apps, and that those who were gay were twice as likely to say they'd used them – much higher figures than in Pew's last study.

Because these apps usually work through geo-navigation – showing who is close by as a central feature – it becomes easier to trace and target people when everyone is confined at home. It was this feature that led to a series of outings in Morocco during April and May.

In Morocco, one of the 70-plus countries where being gay is still illegal, a social media

When you are gay in Morocco you learn to not trust each other. Secrecy is in the culture

influencer and model Sofia Talouni used quarantine to ask people to join dating sites and out men they might know.

"You might find someone who is 200, 100 metres away. You might even find someone half a metre from you, in your living room or in your bedroom," said Talouni, urging the outings via her Instagram Live feed.

Up to 100 men in Morocco have since been harassed and abused, with reports that some have been kicked out of their homes. One has taken his own life.

In countries where being gay is either illegal or socially unacceptable, the use of such apps can be a matter of life or death. And these hate crimes appear to be on the rise during the coronavirus restrictions.

South Korea's LGBTQ community is reporting a spike in homophobic incidents after a cluster of coronavirus cases were connected to clubs frequented by the country's gay community. Local media called for the identities of all of those who visited the clubs to be revealed at the same time as many reported receiving hate speech on gay dating app Grindr.

Despite South Korea's outwardly modern image, it remains a deeply traditional society and homophobia is rife, even though same-sex relationships are not illegal.

"Many queer people are afraid that their visit to Itaewon [the area of Seoul where the nightclubs were] will be known... The stigma towards the disease and sexual minority threatens their lives," said Bak Gi-Jin, a spokesperson from Queer Action against Covid-19 in South Korea.

"Because of patriarchal family culture and institutions, many queer people do not come out until they are completely independent from their parents," she added. "As outing can be deadly to sexual minorities, most of them hide their sexual identity in their workplace."

She said one company had even announced on its digital job advert that gay men could not apply.

In Russia, the situation is particularly dire.

"Many Russians believe that the virus was spread by the LGBT community or that it

ABOVE: A man, who
lost his job after
being arrested for
showing affection
to a member of the
same sex in public,
walks with a friend
along a train track in
Lagos, Nigeria, 14
February 2020

was a punishment for their sins," said Yulia
Tsvetkova, a Russian activist who won the
2020 Index on Censorship Freedom of Expression arts award.

Tsvetkova isn't just worried about the present – she's worried about the future.

"We will soon have a change in the country's
constitution, which will make the situation for
the Russian LGBT community even worse, so
I am afraid," she said in reference to Vladimir
Putin's proposal for a constitutional ban on

gay marriage (something that should have been
voted on in April). This is in a country where
the murder of gay people is already neither
unusual nor concealed. Last year, for example,
LGBTQ activist Yelena Grigoryeva was fatally
stabbed in St Petersburg after her name was
listed on a website that encouraged people to
"hunt" LGBTQ activists.

Tsvetkova receives regular death threats and
is currently under house arrest, banned from
communicating with anyone except her mother

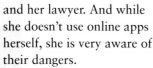

and her lawyer. And while she doesn't use online apps herself, she is very aware of their dangers.

"I know that sometimes homophobes set up provocations when they meet an LGBT person online and ask for a meeting in person. After that they film the 'date' and then blackmail an LGBT person, threatening that otherwise they will tell on [them]."

She said they also often monitored dating apps, outing people on social media.

Index spoke to Samir El Mouti, the director of an NGO that campaigns against violence towards LGBTQ people in Morocco through a Facebook group, The Moroccan LGBT Community. El Mouti is largely forthcoming, partly because he's now studying for a PhD in Edinburgh and feels reasonably safe, he says. Still, there's an air of caution during our initial conversation.

"We don't know if these pages are safe," he said of the Facebook group when speaking over the phone. "When you are gay in Morocco you learn to not trust each other. Secrecy is in the culture."

El Mouti says people are cautioned against putting up their real photos. While he is not sure if the government monitors the sites, if anyone is caught on these sites they're "screwed" because the law discriminates rather than protects people.

In India, similar stories have circulated. Despite a landmark ruling in 2018 legalising gay sex, the LGBTQ community faces regular stigma and violence. And, as in Morocco, those who suffer harassment have very few spaces where they can speak up and out.

As outing can be deadly to sexual minorities, most of them hide their sexual identity in their workplace

Privacy issues and safety concerns have plagued LGBTQ dating apps from the get-go. Grindr, the world's largest, has gone from scandal to scandal since it was launched in 2009.

In 2016, for example, it faced scrutiny when a Daily Beast reporter used Grindr to uncover how much sexual activity took place in the Olympic Village, exposing the sexual identities of athletes.

In 2018, reports emerged of a security issue that could expose users' precise locations. That same year, it was revealed that the app had shared data on its users' HIV status with third parties.

These are just the examples that make headlines. Index has spoken to people from Chile to China and it is always the same story. Yes, people use apps; no, they're really not secure.

Some believe these dating apps can be a safe haven. "Grindr has been so useful as a way of lessening the loneliness of this moment. Having private spaces are such a luxury. You're able to be yourself and you're able to connect," said Rohit K Dasgupta, an academic who edited the book Queering Digital India: Activisms, Identities, Subjectivities.

But just how prolific are fake accounts? Catfishing – when someone creates a fictional persona online to lure someone else – is rampant on gay dating apps.

"I have lost count of the amount of times a friend has contacted me to show me a Grindr profile using my photograph that is blatantly not me," Glaswegian writer Jonathan Morris told Index, also listing examples of men he's met who used fake online photos.

Posing as someone you're not might be a way for the less attractive to find a date, but it can also be used as a way to abuse people on these platforms, with some extreme incidents involving violence – sometimes murder. →

I have lost count of the amount of times a friend has contacted me to show me a Grindr profile using my photograph

→ Aware of both their popularity and their safety issues, app makers have tried to come up with ways to enhance privacy without jeopardising user experience. In many ways they're stuck between a rock and a hard place. Some have tried to improve verification measures, such as Hornet, which has 25 million users worldwide.

But going down the "blue tick badge" route offers protection to some users at the expense of others. What if governments or hackers accessed whole databases of sexual minorities?

"Not everyone wants to, or even should, be identified," said Eric Silverberg, chief executive of dating app Scruff, in an interview with the BBC.

Hinge, for example, now automatically deletes all communications the moment users delete their accounts. Scruff enables users to easily flag offending accounts within the app, and claims to respond to all complaints within 24 hours.

And Grindr – which did not respond to requests to comment from Index – has just launched a new app, Grindr Lite, specifically for people living in countries where being out is difficult.

It features a Discreet App icon, which gives users the ability to disguise the famous logo on their phones as something less conspicuous, as well as a feature to hide their distance from other users. (See also our report in Index 48.03 on Tinder introducing a feature for users to hide their profiles when travelling to countries where homosexuality is criminalised.)

But there is a strong sense that app providers still need to do a lot more, especially right now.

"Some platforms require you to post a face picture with a code (Dudesnude), when you first create a profile to ensure you are legitimate, but that's not something that has been carried over onto the apps," said Morris.

This all means that safety is up to the users and society at large.

But el Mouti identifies at least one positive trend. While he has little faith Morocco's laws will change, he takes comfort in some people becoming more supportive.

"People are starting to realise these are people who have been discriminated against for a long time," he said. "The mentality is changing." ⊗

Jemimah Steinfeld *is deputy editor of Index on Censorship*